A GUIDED TOUR OF THE
COLLECTED WORKS
OF C. G. JUNG

A C. G. JUNG FOUNDATION BOOK

The C. G. Jung Foundation for Analytical Psychology is dedicated to helping men and women grow in conscious awareness of the psychological realities in themselves and society, find healing and meaning in their lives and greater depth in their relationships, and live in response to their discovered sense of purpose. It welcomes the public to attend its lectures, seminars, films, symposia, and workshops and offers a wide selection of books for sale through its bookstore. The Foundation also publishes *Quadrant,* a semi-annual journal, and books on Analytical Psychology and related subjects. For information about Foundation programs or membership, please write to the C. G. Jung Foundation, 28 East 39th Street, New York, NY 10016.

A GUIDED TOUR OF THE
COLLECTED WORKS
OF C. G. JUNG

ROBERT H. HOPCKE

SHAMBHALA
BOSTON & LONDON
1999

TO MY FAMILY

Shambhala Publications, Inc.
Horticultural Hall
300 Massachusetts Avenue
Boston, Massachusetts 02115
http://www.shambhala.com

©1989, 1999 by Robert H. Hopcke

9 8 7 6 5 4 3 2 1

Second Edition

Printed in the United States of America

⊗ This edition is printed on acid-free paper that meets the American National Standards Institute Z39.48 Standard.

Distributed in the United States by Random House, Inc., and in Canada by Random House of Canada Ltd.

The Library of Congress catalogues the first edition of this work as follows:

Hopcke, Robert, 1958–
    A guided tour of the collected works of C. G. Jung/Robert H. Hopcke; foreword by Aryeh Maidenbaum.—1st ed.
        pp.   cm.
    Bibliography: p.
    ISBN 0-87773-470-4
    ISBN 0-87773-582-4 (paper)
    ISBN 1-57062-405-4 (1999 paper ed.)
    1. Jung, C. G. (Carl Gustav, 1875–1961).   2. Psychoanalysis.
    1. Title.
    BF173.j85H66   1989   88-34345
    150.19'54—dc19   CIP

CONTENTS

ACKNOWLEDGMENTS

While the idea for a book and its writing may belong to an author, the labor of making a book a reality could not be accomplished without a great deal of help and support. Many thanks are due to the woman who urged me to read Jung and went out of her way to enable me to do so, Dorlesa Barmettler-Ewing of California State University, Hayward; under her Swiss direction my acquaintance with the *Collected Works* first took place and deepened over the years. Those connected with the C. G. Jung Institute of San Francisco who have lent a helping hand are also due great thanks: Scott Wirth, Karin Carrington, Rita Cahn, Carol Tuttle, John Beebe, and Raymond Kilduff all have contributed directly and indirectly to my being able to put form to this formlessness. Joan Alpert, the June Institute librarian, and the library volunteers are to be recognized for their invaluable interest, support, and encouragement throughout the research process. Members of the Analytical Psychology Club of Berkeley, especially Celia Correa and Daniel DeYoung, have helped me understand Jung more clearly and in a more immediate way through being able to share our own inner lives with each other in the course of numerous discussions. The folks connected with Shambhala Publications, without whom this book would never have been, I acknowledge with much gratitude and affection: Kimn Nielson, Jonathan Green, and Emily Hilburn Sell all share in the midwifery of this volume. Finally, those with whom I share my life are to be congratulated for bearing with me and providing a place of rest, relaxation, and fun in the midst of the sometimes grueling work this book entailed: Gery Short and Roseann Alexander, Mark Castillo and Jennifer Diaz, Dan Fee, Jill Johnson, and, with much love, Paul Schwartz.

A GUIDED TOUR OF THE
COLLECTED WORKS
OF C. G. JUNG

INTRODUCTION

This book is written in response to many stimuli, some personal, some collective. On the personal level, I find myself in a number of roles as practicing psychotherapist: healer, teacher, supervisor, mentor, writer, reader, patient in analysis, and analyst of others. In nearly all of these roles I have been exposed to what one might call a groundswell of interest in the writings of C. G. Jung. My clients are interested in Jung's ideas and find Jungian-oriented dream work both challenging and nourishing. My students in workshops and case seminars want to know more about Jung's theories on subjects not usually associated with Jungian thought, such as homosexuality, narcissism, object relations and developmental theory, group therapy. My supervisees pump me on the uses of Jung's more practical concepts in their work with their clients, for example, his theory of psychological types, his methods of dream analysis, his understanding of spiritual growth.

Others in the field know of my interest in Jung through my writing and ask me for elucidation of some of his more difficult concepts such as synchronicity, the nature of the archetypes, the Self. I attempt to read as much as possible in the ever growing literature on Jung's ideas, and my reading stimulates my writing as I discover new connections in Jung's thought by filtering his thought through my experience. Again and again I find myself using Jung's conceptions to make sense of my actions and interactions with others, my shadow projections, my complexes, my alluring archetypal images.

On the collective level, the reasons that Jung and his writ-

1

ings have become more interesting to more people than ever before are open to conjecture. Perhaps psychology as a field is not so keenly gripped by its inferiority complex as a natural science and so the field no longer needs to prove itself through a slavish devotion to rationality. The waning of Freudian psychoanalytic influence and the increasingly irrelevant aridity of experimental psychology seem to be twin results of an awareness that psychology as rational science, as an objective and impartial body of knowledge, is a myth. The threat of global extinction, one result of this myth of rationality, may have at last forced upon human beings an inward turn of the intellect, a penitential soul-searching, in order to understand ourselves and find the courage and hope we need to survive our own aggression. And let us not forget the patent symbol of the millennium that forces a certain pervasive consciousness of what it means to be human. At such a juncture, Jung and his work on the meaning and purpose of myths would appear useful in finding the necessary way forward, the *tertium non datur,* between psychoanalysis and behaviorism.

Certainly much of the revival of interest in Jung's writing is due to Jungian analysts, particularly those now one generation removed from the person of C. G. Jung, who have begun to cast their nets of observation wider and wider. As Jungian analysts gain distance from the figure of Jung himself, perhaps the professional cliquishness of the Jungian "inner circle" has given way to the realization of how relevant Jung is to all modern individuals, not just Jungian "believers." And the result of this widening of scope in the last decade has been to make Jung and Jungian thought "popular"—the focus of best-selling books, public television series, sold-out workshops and talks by internationally known speakers. However, the commercial success of such books, shows, and events comes with a price. As Jung's thought has been popularized, it has often been distorted, his ideas simplified, his views misrepresented (sometimes with the lamentably obvious intention of fomenting controversy in order to boost sales). Various of the more egregious distortions one hears could be easily set right, if one would only read Jung's own writings thoughtfully and carefully rather than relying on interpretations of Jung put forward by people with biases in either direction.

But here a difficulty arises. For instance, someone, not necessarily an analyst or a therapist, wants to know more about Jung's ideas of archetypes of the collective unconscious. Where does one go? Which articles should one read? One faces the twenty volumes of Jung's *Collected Works* and the sight is daunting. Which volume to pick? Which paper in which volume? Though the groupings of the papers and the titles of the volumes are helpful, one risks finding oneself face to face with a piece of Jung's more esoteric or incomprehensible writings. Jung, after all, did not write with the intention of putting together a coherent theoretical system. Many people, I have found, do not take the risk of attempting the *Collected Works* and some others who do often end up in frustration.

One compromise is to read some sort of general overview of Jung's writings, ostensibly before actually reading Jung. Thus, the educated layperson turns away from Jung's writings and instead toward the general expositions of Jungian psychology that so many analysts have provided. The problem here is not that these overviews are bad, but, on the contrary, that they are so uniformly good. In fact, my experience has been that the clarity and helpfulness of these general expositions often is such that many people never go on to the next logical step, that is, reading Jung's own writing. One has the sense of having understood Jung, although one may never have actually read through any of Jung's more important writings in their entirety.

For the educated layperson or for a client in Jungian-oriented therapy, a profound scholarly grasp of Jung's own

writings is not required. Many of Jung's concepts are quite understandable and down to earth, not at all esoteric or arcane,
since, with his typical Swiss penchant for practicality, he viewed
theories as tools, aids toward understanding. The real problem
in never reading Jung, in never really tackling the *Collected
Works*, is rather the way in which one loses the living experience
of reading a great thinker of twentieth-century Western civilization. This book sets out to correct such a loss.

The curious notion that to read a volume of the *Collective
Works* will require untold academic effort and years of study is
not true. The idea that Jung is hard to read, that he did not
write well, or that his German does not translate well into English is also not true, nor is the notion that Jung's writing is
disorganized, haphazard, and intuitive and so does not make
sense.

The reality is that much, if not all, of Jung's writing is accessible to a general readership if one were to have a brief introduction to a concept as Jung uses it and if one were to know
which writings to begin with and which to save for later. The
purpose of this book is therefore to provide a topically organized introduction to the wide variety of Jung's theoretical concepts and a planned set of readings around each concept
under examination—in essence, a guided tour of the *Collected
Works*.

The metaphor of the guided tour truly describes the purpose of this book, which is intended to serve the way a Michelin
or Baedeker guide serves the European tourist: to provide
enough orientation and historical information to enable one
to understand what one sees, to direct one's gaze here and not
there, and to put in one's hand an aid toward greater knowledge and experience. One might use this book profitably to
read through just those pieces of Jung's writing which, for whatever reason, pique one's interest or raise one's hackles. On the
other hand, one might use this book as a program of study—

personal, professional, or academic—to achieve a thorough-going knowledge of what Jung wrote. In either case, the purpose in providing this guided tour of the *Collected Works* is not to supplant previous expositions of Jungian psychology nor to augment the already plentiful supply of research tools. Another tome certainly does not need to be thrown upon the heap of books already written *about* Jung's theories. Rather, the purpose is to help interested people gain entrance into Jung's writings and, through these writings, glimpse the heart and soul of Jung's thought.

The format of this guided tour is in keeping with its purpose, which is to help people read through the *Collected Works*. This book is divided into four parts—"The Ways and Means of the Psyche," "Archetypal Figures," "Topics of Special Interest," and "Esoterica"—which are based on the various focuses of Jung's writings. The first two sections, "Ways and Means" and "Archetypal Figures," cover what most people would consider the bulk of Jung's psycyology. The section "Topics of Special Interest" refers to writings in the *Collected Works* that are not generally considered of primary significance but that are interesting and at times quite provocative. The section "Esoterica" covers writings on topics of extreme academic interest or depth that the ordinary reader might not be particularly prone to read. These last two categories of Jung's writings are important to know, however, since they show Jung's breadth of interest, which reached far beyond the realm of what most people would consider academic psychology.

Each of these sections is organized topically, and the topics are arranged so as to build on the material covered in the previous topic. The topical organization of the book comes from my experience, which is that one is rarely drawn into Jung's writings through a desire to know Jung in all his theoretical complexity. More often, I have found, one or two of his ideas resonate within one's experience and lead one to want to know and read more. For me, the magnet that compelled me to read Jung was his conception of the dream and of dream analysis. For others I have known, the magnet has been his notions of synchronicity, the collective unconscious, individuation, anima/animus, and, of course, archetypes.

Each of the topic sections begins with a short theoretical discussion of the concept in question, followed by four categories of readings in or about the *Collected Works:*

1. *To Begin.* These are articles or works in the *Collected Works* that are easiest to read first and treat the topic in question at some length.

2. *To Go Deeper.* These are articles or works in the *Collected Works* that are a bit more difficult, usually require a certain amount of study, and are necessary to read for a complete understanding of the topic.

3. *Related Works.* These are articles or works by Jung that are in some way related to the topic in question and put the concept in the context of Jung's thought. At times, other topics in this guided tour may be indicated because of their closeness to the topic in question.

4. *Secondary Sources.* These are books (or at times articles in collections) by Jungians or others that are considered significant works on the subject, chosen here with an eye for accessibility. These lists are not meant as comprehensive bibliographies. While the scholar may wish to read dense, thorough treatments of the topics or consult hard-to-find journals available only at Jungian training institutes, the lay reader will wish to augment his or her understanding using books that are for the most part still in print and available, at least by order, through a

local bookstore, and that are fairly easy to read. Most of the secondary sources listed fit this criterion. In addition, I have listed a mixture of both first-generation sources and contemporary writers whenever possible, while keeping the list short and to the point.

The topical organization of the book is intended to carry through my fundamental purpose, which is to aid the nonspecialist in beginning to read the *Collected Works*. To this end, the theoretical introductions are as comprehensive as necessary but as brief as possible. Jung's writings are the primary focus here; my interpretations of his concepts are meant only as an orientation to what might be unfamiliar to the general reader.

One will notice that certain articles or works are mentioned under several topics. Many of Jung's writings tied many of his own notions together in a unique way, and so reading the whole work as written by Jung, whether it is a short article or an entire book, will reveal connections and interconnections one might otherwise miss. I have honored Jung's writings by recommending only whole works but have attempted to keep the repetitions to a minimum by indicating the most salient major parts of those works according to the topic in question. Since many readers will choose to use this book selectively, rather than go from cover to cover, the unavoidable repetition of reading suggestions may not be tiresome after all. Furthermore, reading the same article from a number of different perspectives is an experience, I venture to say, almost required for the full effect of Jung's ideas to sink in. To read and reread Jung, to study and spend time with him, to come back to the same place again and again with fresh insights or with different questions is probably the best way to Jung.

As the format makes clear, this book is not intended to serve so much as a reference work as a planned program, a guided tour, for reading the *Collected Works*. The reader interested in becoming familiar with only a few of Jung's concepts is directed to the table of contents, which will aid in locating particular topics. However, this book will be most useful for people who wish to be familiar with the *Collected Works* as a whole but who find the twenty silent black volumes too formidable to open without encouragement or direction.

There are numerous general overviews of Jung by major Jungian writers which provide their own summation of analytical psychology's basic concepts. Six of the best known and most used are: M. Esther Harding, *The "I" and the "Not I"* (New York: Pantheon Books, 1965); Jolande Jacobi, *The Psychology of C. G. Jung* (New Haven: Yale University Press, 1973); June Singer, *Boundaries of the Soul* (New York: Doubleday, 1973); Marie-Louise von Franz, *C. G. Jung: His Myth in Our Time* (New York: C. G. Jung Foundation for Analytical Psychology, 1975); Edward Whitmont, *The Symbolic Quest: Basic Concepts in Analytical Psychology* (Princeton: Princeton University Press, 1978); and Frances G. Wickes, *The Inner World of Man,* second edition (Boston: Sigo Press, 1988). For the reader merely interested in the definitions of major concepts in analytical psychology, as well as Jungian interpretations of other psychological concepts, *The Critical Dictionary of Jungian Analysis,* edited by Samuels, Shorter, and Plaut (New York: Routledge & Kegan Paul, 1986), is highly recommended. For those interested in reading excerpts of Jung's writings organized by topic, *The Essential Jung,* edited by Anthony Storr (Princeton: Princeton University Press, 1983), will be helpful. Finally, there is the unique and entertaining overview of Jungian psychology contained in the volume *Man and His Symbols* (Garden City, N.Y.: Doubleday, 1964), to which Jung and four of his colleagues contributed.

For those readers who have already used this book over the last ten years as a way to enter into a direct encounter with Jung, I would like to extend both thanks and reassurance. Though this second edition is indeed updated, the only revision has been to the list of secondary sources at the end of each section. Many holes in the Jungian literature have been filled expertly and abundantly since this book's original publication; topics for which there was little or nothing when I first wrote are now their own field of study. This second edition reflects this abundance, while all references here to Jung and the *Collected Works* remained untouched.

PART ONE

THE WAYS AND MEANS
OF THE PSYCHE

1. ARCHETYPES AND THE COLLECTIVE UNCONSCIOUS

Jung himself called his psychological theory *analytical psychology*, both to express its direction and to distinguish his approach from Freud's psychoanalysis. However, many writers and psychologists have found that the term *archetypal psychology* is almost a more apt description, and, indeed, this term points to perhaps the most fundamental and distinctive concept in analytical psychology: that of the archetypes of the collective unconscious.

To separate Jung's conception of the archetype from his theory of the collective unconscious is impossible. Each depends on the other for theoretical coherence. One could not speak of archetypes, as Jung used the term, without the theory of the collective unconscious, nor could the collective unconscious truly be collective, as Jung used the term, without the archetypes. Therefore, the concepts are treated here as two parts of a single theory.

The term *archetype* is not coined by Jung, and Jung points out its origin in patristic writings as an "explanatory paraphrase of the Platonic *eidos*" (cw 9, I, p. 4). Jung's unique contribution was to use the idea of archetype in a psychological sense with reference to contemporary people. Archetypes were for him "typical modes of apprehension" (cw 8, p. 137)—that is, patterns of psychic perception and understanding common to all human beings as members of the human race.

Jung came to posit the existence of such common modes

of apprehension by way of *empirical* observation. His broad knowledge of mythology, anthropological material, religious systems, and ancient art allowed him to see that the symbols and figures that continually appeared in many of his patients' dreams were identical to symbols and figures that had appeared and reappeared over thousands of years in myths and religions all over the world. Moreover, Jung frequently found himself at a loss to trace the appearance of such symbols in his patients' dreams to experiences in the patients' individual lives.

Jung thus broadened and deepened Freud's conception of the unconscious. Rather than being simply the repository of repressed personal memories or forgotten experiences, the unconscious, it seemed to Jung, consisted of two parts or layers. The first layer, which he called the personal unconscious, was basically identical to Freud's conception of the unconscious. In this layer of the unconscious lay the memories of everything that an individual had experienced, thought, felt, or known but that was now no longer held in active awareness, whether through defensive repression or because of simple forgetting.

However, in using his theory of archetypes to account for similarities in psychic functioning and imagery throughout the ages and across highly diverse cultures, Jung conceived of a second layer of the unconscious, which he called the collective unconscious. This layer of the unconscious was the layer that contained those patterns of psychic perception common to all humanity, the archetypes. Because the collective unconscious was the realm of archetypal experience, Jung considered the collective unconscious layer deeper and ultimately more significant than the personal unconscious. To become aware of the figures and movements of the collective unconscious brought one into direct contact with essential human experiences and perceptions, and the collective unconscious was considered by Jung to be the ultimate psychic source of power, wholeness, and inner transformation.

Though the concepts of archetypes and the collective unconscious were frequently attacked as philosophical speculation and idle theorizing, Jung continually maintained that his assertion of the existence of this level of the human psyche was scientifically supportable on the basis of empirical evidence.

Another common misunderstanding of the concept of archetypes, besides the charge that it is unscientific, is the confusion between the content of the archetype and the archetype itself. The archetype itself is neither an inherited idea nor a common image. A better description is that the archetype is like a psychic mold into which individual and collective experiences are poured and where they take shape, yet it is distinct from the symbols and images themselves. In this sense, Jung's concept of the archetype is the psychological counterpart of Plato's form, or *eidos*.

Nevertheless, the confusion between the content of the archetype and the archetype itself is understandable since particular archetypes are referred to by their symbolic or imaginal manifestations. Jung talks about the archetypes of the anima/animus, the Divine Child, the Great Mother, the Wise Old Man, the Trickster, and the Kore, or Maiden—archetypes whose content is anthropomorphic and whose personalization is necessary in order to bring the psychological power of the pattern into consciousness for greater awareness and individual growth. Yet there are archetypes whose content is less anthropomorphic, less readily personalized, such as the archetype of wholeness or the archetype of rebirth. These archetypes Jung called archetypes of transformation, "typical situations, places, ways and means, that symbolize the kind of transformation in question" (cw 9, I, p. 38).

Jung saw the archetypes as ambivalent, potentially positive and negative. Insofar as the archetypes themselves are, by definition, outside of conscious awareness, they function autonomously, almost as forces of nature, organizing human experience for the individual in particular ways without regard to the constructive or destructive consequences to the individual life. Psychological growth occurs only when one attempts to bring the content of the archetypes into conscious awareness and establish a relationship between one's conscious life and the archetypal level of human existence.

The references that follow include Jung's major expositions of these concepts. The concept of the archetype, however, is more comprehensively grasped by becoming familiar with the various archetypal figures and patterns that are the exclusive focus of the second part of this book. Therefore, these references focus mainly on Jung's theories of the unconscious, which are inseparable from his conception of the archetype.

To Begin

"The Concept of the Collective Unconscious," cw 9, I, pp. 42–53.

"Archetypes of the Collective Unconscious," cw 9, I. pp. 3–41.

"The Relations Between the Ego and the Unconscious," cw 7, esp. pp. 127–138.

To Go Deeper

"On the Psychology of the Unconscious," cw 7, esp. pp. 64–113.

"The Structure of the Psyche," cw 8, pp. 139–158.

"On the Nature of the Psyche," cw 8, pp. 159–234.

"The Role of the Unconscious," cw 10, pp. 3–28.

"The Tavistock Lectures," cw 18, esp. Lecture 2, pp. 36–69.

Related Works

"The Significance of the Unconscious in Individual Education," cw 17, pp. 149–164.

"Conscious, Unconscious and Individuation," cw 9, I, pp. 275–289.

Secondary Sources

Jacobi, Jolande. *Complex/Archetype/Symbol in the Psychology of C. G. Jung*. Princeton: Princeton University Press, 1959.

Neumann, Erich. *The Origins and History of Consciousness*. Princeton: Princeton University Press, 1954.

2. COMPLEX

Closely allied with Jung's concept of archetype and the collective unconscious is his concept of the complex, which he formulated on the basis of empirical evidence and which proved somewhat less controversial. While working at the Burghölzli Hospital in Zurich as a young man, he undertook the development of a word association test as a means of detecting the unconscious roots of mental illness. Exceedingly simple in design, the test consisted of presenting a word to the test subject and then soliciting a spontaneous verbal response to that word. Examination of a subject's responses, both verbal and nonverbal, seemed to indicate what Jung first called "emotionally charged complexes" (cw 2, p. 72n.), and later a "feeling-toned complex of ideas" in the unconscious (cw 2, p. 321), which hindered the normal course of word association and which was clearly related to the patient's pathology. These feeling-toned complexes, later simply called complexes, in Jung's view consist of two components: the group of psychic representations and the distinctive feeling attached to that group of representations.

Complexes may be unconscious—repressed due to the painfulness of the related affect or unacceptability of the representations—but complexes can also be made conscious and at least partially resolved. Any one complex has elements related to the personal unconscious as well as to the collective unconscious. A disturbed relationship to one's mother, for example, may result in a mother complex, that is, a group of representations, conscious and unconscious, of "mother" with a particular feeling tone attached to that group of mother images. However, the preexisting archetype of "mother" in the collective unconscious common to all human experience can magnify, distort, or modify both the feeling tone and the representational aspect of the mother complex within one's psyche.

Like the archetypes, complexes are potentially both positive and negative. Conscious knowledge of the scope and affect of a complex can serve to modify its negative consequences whenever a particular stimulus constellates the complex, that is, activates the images and feelings surrounding the complex within an individual. All complexes have an archetypal component, making them, in Jung's terms, the *via regia* to the personal and collective unconscious (CW 8, p. 101). In giving image to this concept of the complex, one could say a complex is like a plant, part of which exists and flowers above the ground, in awareness, and part of which extends unseen beneath the ground, where it is anchored and fed, outside of awareness.

To Begin

"Psychoanalysis and the Association Experiments," CW 2, pp. 288–317.

"The Psychological Diagnosis of Evidence," CW 2, pp. 318–352.

"The Psychopathological Significance of the Association Experiment," CW 2, pp. 408–425.

"A Review of the Complex Theory," CW 8, pp. 92–104.

To Go Deeper

"Association, Dream and Hysterical Symptom," CW 2, pp. 353–407.

"The Family Constellation," CW 2, pp. 466–479.

"The Psychological Foundation of Belief in Spirits," CW 8, p. 301.

Related Works

"On the Nature of the Psyche," cw 8, pp. 159–234.

"On Psychic Energy," cw 8, pp. 3–66.

"Psychological Aspects of the Mother Archetype," cw 9, I, pp. 75–110.

Secondary Sources

Jacobi, Jolande. *Complex/Archetype/Symbol in the Psychology of C. G. Jung.* Princeton: Princeton University Press, 1959.

3. LIBIDO

To understand the psychoanalytic use of the term *libido* requires that one understand one of the fundamental ideas of depth psychology, one of its basic and most revolutionary metaphors: the psyche as a dynamic system. Rather than think of the psyche, or mind, as consisting of a static group of fixed components, Freud, Jung, and many other psychologists at the beginning of the twentieth century found a closer parallel with the idea of the mind as a kind of complicated internal mechanism, regulating and adjusting the flow of thoughts and emotions to assure adequate reality perception and proper functioning. Though this model is itself mechanistic if taken too literally, the psychologists who adopted this newer, psychodynamic model found themselves freed from the truly materialistic bias of early European psychological research, which had reduced all mind functions to simple biological or neurological processes. In rejecting this neurobiological conception of the mind, Freud, Jung, and all their associates came to appreciate that the psyche is actually an ever moving, ever changing set of interrelationships, greater than the sum of its parts and always active, though at times this activity may be out of awareness, or unconscious.

In elaborating this new model of psychic functioning, Freud borrowed the term *libido* from the Latin to describe the fuel on which this psychic system ran, the drive energy that came to be repressed, channeled, displaced, or sublimated by the various psychological processes Freud discovered. In positing that sexual conflicts were the psychological cause of neurosis, however, Freud came to use the term *libido* in a considerably restricted sense, to denote sexual energy in particular, and this usage of the term in psychoanalysis as well as in everyday parlance is nowadays its most common one.

Jung found that this term was "very suitable for practical usage" (CW 7, p. 52, n. 6) but felt that an exclusive usage of the term to connote sexual energy was too narrow and not in keeping with the original Latin meaning of the word as desire, longing, urge (CW 8, p. 30, n. 47). Thus, in rejecting Freud's overweening emphasis on sexuality, Jung writes, "libido for me means psychic energy, which is the equivalent to the intensity with which psychic contents are charged" (CW 7, pp. 52–53, n. 6), a much more neutral use of the term, in line with Jung's general theory of the psyche as a dynamic phenomenon.

Further, Jung's use of the term *libido* is broader than Freud's because Jung's conception of the psyche is also broader than that of orthodox Freudian psychoanalysis. In moving beyond the idea that the mind is simply a push-pull of drive and defense with libido as the grease, Jung used *libido* to describe something more ineffable and mysterious, libido as defined by its results or effects. For example, the attention one devotes to inner or outer objects, the fluid magnetism that exists between people, the attraction to particular qualities or things, that quality of action which one might call colloquially one's get up and go, the ability to get things done—all these are the various shades of meaning that this simple term had in Jung's thought. These connotations clearly push the term *libido* somewhat beyond its strict definition as emotional charge toward the common Jungian usage of the word to mean psychic energy, rendering the term as flexible and potent linguistically as libido is itself within the psyche.

Jung's revision of the libido theory first appeared in *Symbols of Transformation,* published in 1912, while Jung was still associated with Freud. As one might imagine, this book with its radical reinterpretations of many of Freud's own concepts, including libido, presaged the famous break between the men which was to occur in 1913, and as such, caused something of a stir on its appearance. The first article in the list that follows was written by Jung as a response to critics of his revision of the concept of libido and therefore has a coherent and concise focus that might enable the first-time reader to grasp Jung's ideas concerning this term. The other articles flesh out Jung's use of the concept. The relevant parts from *Symbols of Transformation* are noted but are probably best read as part and parcel of the entire book, rather than as excerpts.

To Begin

"On Psychic Energy," cw 8, pp. 3–66.

To Go Deeper

"The Theory of Psychoanalysis," cw 4, pp. 83–226, esp. chap. 3, "The Concept of Libido," pp. 111–128.

"Psychoanalysis and Neurosis," cw 4, pp. 243-251.

"Freud and Jung: Contrasts," cw 4, pp. 333–340.

Symbols of Transformation, cw 5, esp. part 1, chap. 3–5, pp. 34–117, and part 2, chaps. 2–3, pp. 132–170.

Related Works

"Instinct and the Unconscious," cw 8, pp. 129–138.

Secondary Sources

Harding, M. Esther. *Psychic Energy: Its Source and Its Transformation.* Princeton: Princeton University Press, 1973.

4. DREAMS AND DREAM INTERPRETATION

Unarguably the cornerstone of Jungian psychology and analytic technique, dream interpretation is one of the most influential contributions Jung has made to modern psychological thought and practice. For this reason, a thorough understanding of the place and character of dream interpretation in Jung's work is vital to understand his psychology as a whole. As one might expect, Jung's methods of dream interpretation are founded on his conception of what a dream is and the psychological function dreams serve.

While heartily agreeing with Freud on the importance of dreams in the analysis of the unconscious, Jung nevertheless disagreed just as heartily with Freud's conception of the dream. For Freud, the dream was a psychological mechanism that functioned to preserve sleep by expressing and thereby discharging unacceptable, unconscious wishes in disguised form. Since in Jung's view the psyche is both a natural and purposive phenomenon, Jung understood dreams likewise, as natural and purposive, the spontaneous, undisguised expressions of unconscious processes. According to Jung, Freud erred in supposing that the reason for our frequent difficulty in laying bare the meaning of a dream is that a disguise is imposed by some putative dream censor. The difficulties we have in interpreting dreams, according to Jung, are due to the unconscious nature of the dream: Dreams do not speak in the verbal or logical language of waking life but rather find their voice in quite a different language, the language of symbolism. To understand dreams, therefore, one must learn to speak this language, the language of the unconscious, with its rich symbols and archetypal imagery.

With regard to Jung's methods of dream interpretation two concepts are important. The first is the idea of association. After a patient would present a dream, Jung would have the patient freely associate to the various symbols or images in the dream as a way of preparing for tentative interpretations of the dream's meaning. As opposed to other popular methods of dream interpretation, which treat dream images as signs to be translated or uncoded, Jung realized that each element of the dream had a symbolic individuality that could best be interpreted by the dreamer and no one else. Thus, Jung gave the *dreamer's* associations to the symbols and images paramount importance.

For example, in using a Jungian approach, to know simply that a woman patient dreamt of a table is not sufficient. What kind of table, old or new, fancy or plain? Was it like any table she had ever seen before, in her own home, at a friend's house? Would she like a table like that in her house or find it clumsy, unsuited to her taste? Gathering such associations to the dream and its contents from the patient first, instead of having the analyst interpret the dream on the basis of preconceived meanings of dream images, is Jung's unique contribution to dream interpretation.

The second concept important to Jung's method of dream work is the idea of symbol amplification. Having gathered the dreamer's associations and made various tentative interpretations of the meaning and purpose of the individual dream, Jung then looked to archetypal parallels for understanding the deeper levels of the dream symbols. Motifs in myths, legends, or folktales which were similar or even identical to those contained in an individual's dream would be helpful in pointing to the archetypal basis of a dream and afford perhaps a more transformative understanding of a dream on the archetypal level.

Jung saw the great majority of dreams functioning in a compensatory way psychologically. By presenting the inner situation of the psyche so as to bring the situation to conscious and integrated awareness within the individual, dreams serve to compensate for what may be missing within one's awareness. Yet Jung did not understand all dreams as compensatory and acknowledged that many dreams function in other ways, such as prospectively, that is, anticipating a psychological direction or development extrasensorily, affording one information about an occurrence outside of the awareness of one's five senses; and prophetically, predicting a future occurrence. These sorts of dreams, however real, are nevertheless rare.

The point of dream work for Jung was to arrive at an interpretation or a set of interpretations that united conscious understanding and unconscious processes in a way that was intellectually, emotionally, and intuitively satisfying. Jung saw that dreams might be interpreted in two ways: objectively, as referring to an outer situation in the dreamer's life, or subjectively, as a representation of the dreamer's inner situation or process. Moreover, as Jung's writings make clear, Jung laid great emphasis on the interpretation of a dream series rather than of any single dream. In a dream series, a set of personal and archetypal dream symbols can be seen to develop, change, and interact with other symbols. Because the language of dreams is imaginal and symbolic, dreams tend to express most fully the workings of the archetypal levels of human consciousness, which can be expressed only symbolically due to its fundamentally psychic nature.

Jung's writings in the *Collected Works* are replete with many detailed dream analyses as well as many theoretical discussions on the method and aim of dream interpretation. Here one feels Jung's clinical work come alive through the enormous subtlety and erudition with which he interprets many impressive and transformative dreams, thus making Jung's dream analyses among the most interesting, and at times most complicated, parts of the *Collected Works*. The readings in the following list are Jung's major statements on dream interpretation as well as some of his more detailed and extensive analyses of various dream series of his patients. These analyses, listed under "Related Works" because Jung's purpose was to illustrate points other than dream interpretation per se, may at times be a bit difficult to read because of their dense imagery and rich interpretations, but they give an accurate sense of how Jung went about dream analysis with his patients.

To complete one's knowledge of Jung's methods of dream interpretation, required reading is *Dream Analysis: Notes of the Seminar Given in 1928–1930*. Circulated in typescript for years among Jungian institutes around the world and kept private because Jung never had time to edit them, these notes were at last published in 1984, making public a storehouse of dream interpretation by Jung and his associates that enormously enriches one's understanding of Jung's methods. Mary Ann Mattoon's book is to be recommended for its excellent organization and practicality, while James Hall's work is both concise and evocative. Each of these books is "must" reading once one has delved into Jung's writings.

To Begin

"The Practical Use of Dream Analysis," cw 16, pp. 139–161.
"General Aspects of Dream Psychology," cw 8, pp. 237–280.
"On the Nature of Dreams," cw 8, pp. 281–297.

To Go Deeper

"The Analysis of Dreams," cw 4, pp. 25–34.
"On the Significance of Number Dreams," cw 4, pp. 48–55.

"Morton Prince: 'The Mechanism and Interpretation of Dreams':
A Critical Review," CW 4, pp. 56–73.

Symbols of Transformation, CW 5, esp. part 1, chap. 2, pp. 7–33.

Related Works

Psychology and Alchemy, CW 12, esp. part 2, pp. 41–223.

"A Study in the Process of Individuation," CW 9, I, pp. 290–354.

Jung, C. G. *Dream Analysis: Notes of the Seminar Given in 1928–1930.*
Princeton: Princeton University Press, 1984.

Secondary Sources

Mattoon, Mary Ann. *Understanding Dreams.* Dallas: Spring Publications, 1984.

Hall, James A. *Jungian Dream Interpretation: A Handbook of Theory and Practice.* Toronto: Inner City Books, 1983.

5. SYMBOL

Although Jung's concept of symbol is central to his psychology, a symbol is perhaps easier to recognize than to define or explain. This curious situation, however, is quite in line with Jung's understanding of symbol as the *best possible representation of something that can never be fully known*. Breaking apart and examining each element of this definition helps shed some light on Jung's particular attention to symbols and on his devotion to creating within his patients the capacity to reflect and live life on a symbolic, not simply a literal, level.

As representations, symbols are the manifestations of archetypes in this world, the concrete, detailed, experiential images that express archetypal constellations of meaning and emotion. But symbols are not identical to the archetypes they represent. While the wand, the phallos, the number three, and the image of Yahweh may all be symbolic of the archetypal masculine, for example, the archetype of the masculine stands apart from these representations. The archetype is the psychic mold of experience, while the symbol is its particular manifestation; the archetypes exist outside of life as we know it as a mode of apperception, while the symbol is drawn from life and points to the archetype beyond our understanding. Thus symbols are essentially what render us human and represent our ability to conceive of that which is beyond our understanding, our capacity for transcending our conscious, embodied state to stand in relation to another supraordinate reality.

As expressions of the unknown and perhaps unknowable, symbols constitute the language of the unconscious, that which is by definition unknown and perhaps unknowable. Examples of how the unconscious speaks through the symbol can be found both in dreams, with their condensed, shifting, multi-level symbolic imagery, and in children's play, a highly symbolic activity carried out by human beings not yet fully aware of their personalities. Because the unconscious expresses itself symbolically, Jung spent a great deal of time researching and explicating symbols, especially symbols that had an archetypal and culturally transformative effect. His idea was that a more comprehensive and subtle understanding of archetypal symbolism would serve to render the unconscious material as conscious as possible and thereby avert the psychologically dangerous situations of one-sidedness or ignorance. Since the symbol points toward something beyond understanding, to experience life symbolically is to touch on the individual meaning in who we are and what we do, the goal of Jung's analytic work.

Jung's writings on the symbol in the *Collected Works* are hard to separate from his writings on dreams and dream interpretation, since his dream interpretations demonstrate in meticulous detail just how Jung conceived of the function of symbolism in our inner and outer lives. Thus, the reader is enjoined to read both Jung's works on the symbol per se and his writings on dreams to achieve a thorough familiarity with this crucial sector of Jung's psychology.

A short note on one of Jung's major works on symbols is in order. The book entitled *Symbols of Transformation,* volume 5 of the *Collected Works,* was written when Jung was associated with Freud and represented Jung's attempt to strike out on a path different from Freud's. Hence the first part of this book is devoted to a reinterpretation of a body of case material published by Theodore Flournoy concerning "Miss Miller"; the second part represents Jung's preliminary attempt to sketch out the process of psychological individuation by way of its symbolism. This book is especially interesting since the present text is an extensive revision Jung performed late in his life, after he had developed and consolidated many ideas now identified as his major contributions to analytical psychology. Thus, *Symbols of Transformation*, volume 5 of the *Collected Works*, is one of the most important to read and become familiar with.

Volume 18, entitled *The Symbolic Life*, is essentially a collection of Jung's writings that should have been included in the other volumes of the *Collected Works* but for various reasons were not. The volume takes its title from a seminar Jung gave in London, and the title piece, along with "Symbols and the Interpretation of Dreams," represents the best and easiest access to Jung's ideas on symbols. Jung's treatments of mandala symbolism may also give the reader the fullest possible sense of just how creative and far-ranging Jung's conception of the symbol could be. The mandala, a symbolic figure used primarily in Asian religious and meditative practice, fascinated Jung as a symbol of wholeness and integration often appearing spontaneously in the dreams and artwork of his analytic patients.

Jung's study of the individuation process, like the Miller fantasies in *Symbols of Transformation*, gives one a hands-on sense of how Jung understood and used a symbolic approach to psychic life and development. The two-volume set of *Visions: Notes of the Seminar Given in 1930–1934* contains invaluable insights into Jung's symbolic approach for those possessing the curiosity and patience to read this freewheeling, image-dense text. Like *Dream Analysis*, mentioned in the previous chapter, these transcripts were long unpublished; they are highly recommended but only after one is already fairly familiar with Jung's ideas and methods.

Jolande Jacobi's brief book gives one a compact theoretical discussion of the symbol in Jungian psychology. Adler's more extensive report of an analytic patient's individuation process in a sense continues Jung's practice of attending to empirical data first and drawing theoretical conclusions later. Winding one's way through the analysis reported in this book may be work but there is no better way to gain an in-depth look at the place of the symbol in Jungian analysis. And finally, the *Encyclopedia of Archetypal Symbolism* should provide the readers with many, many hours of exploration and inspiration. With thousand of images culled from the Archive for Research in Archetypal Symbolism (ARAS) housed at the three Jung Institutes in New York, San Francisco, and Los Angeles, this compendium of archetypal symbols with commentary is a unique and invaluable introduction to the breadth of Jung's attitude and thought on symbols.

To Begin

"The Symbolic Life," CW 18, pp. 267–290.

"Symbols and the Interpretation of Dreams," CW 18, pp. 183–264.

To Go Deeper

Symbols of Transformation, CW 5.

"A Study in the Process of Individuation," CW 9, I, pp. 290–354.

"Concerning Mandala Symbolism," CW 9, I, pp. 355–384.

"Mandalas," CW 9, I, pp. 387–390.

Related Works

Psychology and Alchemy, CW 12, esp. part 2, "Individual Dream Symbolism in Relation to Alchemy," pp. 39–223.

Visions: Notes of the Seminar Given in 1930–1934, 2 vols. Claire Douglas, editor. Princeton: Princeton University Press, 1997.

Secondary Sources

Jacobi, Jolande. *Complex/Archetype/Symbol in the Psychology of C. G. Jung*. Princeton: Princeton University Press, 1959.

Adler, Gerhard. *The Living Symbol: A Case Study in the Process of Individuation*. New York: Pantheon, 1961.

An Encyclopedia of Archetypal Symbolism,

Vol. 1, edited by Beverly Moon (Shambhala Publications, 1991, 1997).

Vol. 2, *The Body,* edited by George Elder (Shambhala Publications, 1996).

6. ACTIVE IMAGINATION

Active imagination was a technique developed by Jung to enhance and develop one's relationship to unconscious material, particularly inner figures that had appeared in dreams or fantasies. With active imagination, Jung intended the individual to take a receptive but active role in encountering and confronting various unconscious archetypal elements within his or her psyche. The activity of active imagination is in contrast to dreaming, which in Jung's view simply occurs. Yet active imagination is not a directive fantasy either, in which the individual pursues the thoughts and wishes of his or her own ego. As Jung developed it, active imagination is intended to straddle the border between passive, receptive awareness of inner unconscious material and active, elective responding to this material in whatever form. June Singer, in her book *Boundaries of the Soul*, calls her chapter on active imagination "Dreaming the Dream Onwards," which is perhaps the best summary description of both the technique and its intent.

In light of Jung's ideas on the nature and function of the psyche, active imagination seems a natural outgrowth of the view that wholeness is a result of making the unconscious conscious and that the psyche is a purposive phenomenon. Active imagination is a way to face more directly the unconscious directions of our inner life while maintaining as far as possible our conscious sense of self and our capacity for informed, ethical action.

As with many of Jung's concepts, active imagination might be better understood through direct experience than through reading about it, since Jung wrote little concerning the conceptual underpinnings of the technique. The most useful and focused discussions of active imagination are indicated in the readings list under "To Begin." In the first, the short essay "The Transcendent Function," Jung describes how consciousness and unconsciousness work in tandem to correct and balance psychic one-sidedness. In this context, Jung goes on to explain how active imagination or fantasy can help transcend or heal the typical split between these two opposite psychic spheres. The second piece is actually the latter half of the fifth of Jung's Tavistock Lectures, a series of talks he gave at the Tavistock Clinic in London in 1935. In response to a question about this technique, Jung expounds on its intention and its effects and launches into a short presentation of material from a patient's fantasy work. Further reading on the topic obviously necessitates going into the various reports of active imaginations which Jung drew from his clinical work, reports that are generally highly detailed and vivid enough to make clear precisely how Jung intended this technique to be used and to what effect. Surely what comes out most clearly in all this material is the value Jung placed on fantasy and his high estimation of its healing function.

The secondary sources are by two noted Jungian analysts. Hannah's book is on active imagination, while Adler's book is primarily a case report of an analysis in which active imagination plays an altogether crucial part. If read together, both serve as a thorough introduction to this vital technique in the armamentarium of Jungian analysis, rounded out by the two more recent works on the topic by Robert Johnson and Verena Kast.

To Begin

"The Transcendent Function," cw 8, pp. 67–91.
"The Tavistock Lectures: On the Theory and Practice of Analytical Psychology," cw 18, esp. Lecture 5, pp. 135–182.

To Go Deeper

"A Study in the Process of Individuation," CW 8, pp. 290–354.

Psychology and Alchemy, CW 12, esp. part 2, pp. 41–223.

Related Works

The Theory of Psychoanalysis, CW 4, esp. chap. 9, I, "Therapeutic Principles of Psychoanalysis," pp. 181–203.

Secondary Sources

Hannah, Barbara. *Encounters with the Soul: Active Imagination as Developed by C. G. Jung.* Santa Monica, Calif.: Sigo Press, 1981.

Adler, Gerhard. *The Living Symbol: A Case Study in the Process of Individuation.* New York: Pantheon, 1961.

Johnson, Robert. *Inner Work: Using Dreams and Active Imagination for Personal Growth.* San Francisco: Harper and Row, 1986.

Kast, Verena. *Imagination as Space of Freedom: Dialogue between the Ego and the Unconscious.* Translated by Anselm Hollo. New York: Fromm, 1993.

7. PSYCHE/SOUL

Jung's concern was rarely to set forth in his writings overarching philosophical definitions of his concepts but instead first and foremost to provide practical expositions of certain aspects of human experience. Nowhere is this more true than when the concept to be elucidated is the very focus and foundation of the discipline of psychology, psyche itself. Thus, in the *Collected Works,* one does not find a theoretical discussion of what psyche is or is not but descriptions of those parts of human experience which Jung found to merit the term *psyche.*

Through his own self-explorations, through his research into the symbolism of human life, and through his clinical work as a psychiatrist, Jung expanded and corrected academic psychology's understanding of *psyche,* which even today is simplistically translated as "mind." Jung's experience with psychic phenomena, especially irrational, unconscious psychic phenomena, led him to take issue with the equation of psyche with mind, an equation he objected to on the grounds that it tends to identify the whole of the psyche with one's consciousness and one's rational powers. The psyche, as understood and elaborated by Jung, is much better seen as the totality of nonphysical life, both rational and irrational, both personal and collective, both conscious and unconscious. This view includes within psyche much more than the narrow physico-rationalistic phenomena understood as psychological before Jung and makes room for those aspects of psyche which go beyond thought or mind, such as sensation, feeling, intuition, and instinct.

Thus, Jung saw psyche as something bigger than the mere personal, ego-identified sense of self; psyche encompasses both consciousness and unconsciousness. For this reason, Jung took to using the word *soul* as the proper modern equivalent of the Greek word *psyche,* and the two terms came to be used largely interchangeably in Jung's writings. For Jung and Jungians, *soul* describes much more evocatively and correctly the vast range of human phenomena that one calls psychic, phenomena that Jung believed to be the true focus of psychology: the individual soul, with its conflicts, heights, depths, and uniqueness; the collective soul, the world soul, one's sense of humanness shared with others; and the transpersonal, supra-individual soul of the metaphysicians and theologians, soul in the spiritual and religious sense, as a manifestation of the mind of God, the objective psyche beyond human understanding.

For this reason, Jung's view of psyche and its equivalence to the concept of soul goes strongly against the grain of many modern psychological approaches, based as they are on the Enlightenment's faith in rationality. This view of psyche relativizes the place of the individual in the cosmic scheme of things and, as Jung's writings indicate, such a relativization of the human being was clearly Jung's conscious intent and his ongoing experience. Psyche, for Jung, is not something within the individual, but rather, more properly speaking, the individual is something that exists within psyche. For many psychologists, Jung's relativization of individual rationality is unacceptable and frightening. However, to see psyche as soul, rather than mind, permits Jung to adopt historical and religious perspectives too often closed down and shut off by other psychological theories. This view of psyche takes seriously one of the distinguishing features of human beings, their symbol-making capacity. Furthermore, despite misguided criticisms of Jung's view, at no point does Jung discount or deny the importance of rational

consciousness as part of psyche, saying rather that there is more
to psyche than meets the modern rational eye.

Jung's writings on psyche, therefore, set out to describe
and delineate with precision and creativity what Heraclitus
(and June Singer) called "the boundaries of the soul." He thus
examines the conscious parts of the psyche—the ego, the sense
of self, psychological types—as well as the unconscious aspects
of psyche—its relationship to instinct, its relationship to choice
and will, the recurrent symbols of psychic functions and human
relationships. He examines psyche and its relationship to religious beliefs and spirituality. He looks at the historical development of psychological consciousness and the effects of its
overvaluation in modern times. He examines psyche's relationship to matter, how psyche and matter are different and how,
at times, they appear as two manifestations of a single reality.
He attempts in his writings a nearly impossible and sometimes
abstruse task: to systematically describe the structure and nature of the psyche while at the same time leaving room for the
living, breathing, developing reality of the soul in all its myriad
individual, collective, and transpersonal manifestations.

Three notes are warranted on the technical terminology
the reader may confront in reading about psyche in the *Collected Works*. First, Jung sometimes uses the word *soul*, particularly in his early writings, in the sense of a part-soul synonymous
with *complex*, an autonomous piece of psychic wholeness that
has broken off, so to speak, and seems to be living a life of
its own. So whereas *psyche* denotes the totality of nonphysical
experience, *soul* may describe but a fragment of that totality in
particular places.

Second, following Jung's early usage, the word *soul*, or *soul-
image*, is at times used as a synonym for the anima as an inner
figure within the psyche. The confusion here is understandable, since *anima* is indeed the Latin word for soul, just as *psyche*
is the Greek term, and *anima* was deliberately chosen by Jung

to express how the anima figure can often represent the psyche itself, a man's soul. In Jung's later writings, however, he came to use *anima* (rather than *soul*) to refer to this inner archetypal figure, but the distinction is often not entirely clear.

Third, Jung uses the term *psychoid* in contradistinction to *psychic* in order to describe that which lies somewhere between the purely psychic and the purely instinctual, a level within which the physical and material mix and mingle, a kind of fused state of the purely gross physical reality of the instinctual drives and its transformation into something higher, the psychization of the instincts, as Jung puts it. These images, feelings, symbols, and experiences are thus not truly psychic but actually better described as psychoid, that is, psychelike, since they are partly nonphysical but also heavily infiltrated with instinctual libido.

These three notes on terminology should demonstrate the slippery and shifting nature of the psyche: whole but fragmented, nonphysical while at times instinctual and psychoid, subjectively experienced and yet an objective reality beyond the mere human subject. Jung's concept and experience of this very object/subject of psychological investigation provides an important correction to the hubris of neurobiological theories of mind or the purely behavioristic thinking of modern-day psychology. The psyche, the soul, is infused with mystery and despite all our attempts continually eludes our cognitive and affective grasp.

To Begin

"Basic Postulates of Analytical Psychology," cw 8, pp. 338–357.

To Go Deeper

"The Structure of the Psyche," cw 8, pp. 139–158.
"On the Nature of the Psyche," cw 8, pp. 159–234.

Related Works

"The Relations between the Ego and the Unconscious," cw 7, pp. 123–241.

Secondary Sources

Von Franz, Marie-Louise. *Projection and Re-Collection in Jungian Psychology: Reflections of the Soul.* London: Open Court, 1981.

Neumann, Erich. *Amor and Psyche: The Psychic Development of the Feminine.* Princeton: Princeton University Press, 1956.

Hillman, James. *The Myth of Analysis: Three Essays in Archetypal Psychology.* New York: Harper & Row, 1972.

Hillman, James. *Re-Visioning Psychology.* New York: Harper & Row, 1975.

8. SPIRIT

In attempting to understand Jung's writings on the spirit, one runs into the same problem as Jung did in his attempt to lay hold of what the word *spirit* denotes. Just as one reaches for one promising explanation, one finds the catch quickly slipping through the clutches of our intellectual net, swimming away into that nettlesome sea of important but hard-to-define aspects of human experience. Jung, therefore, approaches spirit the way he deals with all the many other tantalizing inhabitants of this experiential sea, that is, from his position as psychologist. He is not interested in or, he confesses, capable of furthering philosophical or theological discussions on the nature of spirit. Rather, he turns his view toward the phenomenology of the spirit in psychic life: what spirit shows itself to be and how it is the same as or different from psyche/soul.

Of course, it is virtually impossible for Jung not to get tangled up to a certain extent in the previous philosophical controversies and theological nets that have been cast about concerning spirit. On this score, the translator's note prefacing "The Psychological Foundation of Belief in Spirits" (cw 8, p. 300) is instructive in pointing out—linguistically, as it were—the flexible and multishaded nature of the concept of spirit, *Geist* in German. Nevertheless, Jung brings a certain amount of cognitive order to what threatens to become a vague morass of terminology by noting that, psychologically, spirit has two meanings and uses. One speaks of *a* spirit, in the sense of an individual thing—a ghost, a mood, an apparition, a quality—and one speaks of *the* spirit, in the sense of some collective thing—spirituality, spiritual principles, spiritual wholeness.

This latter sense of the spirit, as the basis for spirituality or certain spiritual principles, Jung leaves by choice to the metaphysicians to debate and discuss. As a psychologist, Jung is much more interested in looking at spirits, in the plural, as manifestations of complexes, spirits as unconscious, archetypally based entities. Because of their roots within the unconscious, these spirits, in the plural, obviously have a relationship to *the* spirit, in the common religious sense, which Jung sees as a part of psyche as soul. But, as usual, Jung is almost always more interested in examining the symbols and imagery of the spirit in psychic life than in propounding theoretical dogma.

Caveat lector, then. Jung's writings on spirit are not for the philosophically or theologically minded, those interested in Hegelian idealism or Christian spirituality. Jung's idea of the spirit will be best seen in his discussions of archetypal imagery of myth, alchemy, and fairy tales ("spirit" stories par excellence) or equally in his treatment of what he called occult phenomena, those uncanny, ghostly, or paranormal occurrences which Jung considered manifestations of psychological complexes. Within these practical discussions of the spirit, Jung touches upon the higher and broader meaning of spirit, and indeed, at various times, he addresses himself more directly to spirit in this larger sense of the term. At all times, however, he speaks of spirit first and foremost as a psychologist interested in looking at the place of the spirit in the workings of the human soul.

Works by Jungians on the spirit are few and far between, if one narrows the field to exclude books on religion or spirituality, of which there are a great number. The best work on the spirit in the sense Jung used the term is found in *Spirit and Nature,* edited by Joseph Campbell, which brings together papers presented at annual Eranos meetings on the shore of Lago Maggiore at Ascona, Switzerland. Two essays of Jung—"The Phenomenology of the Spirit in Fairy Tales" and "The Spirit of Psychology," a piece subsequently retitled "On the Nature of the Psyche" (cw 8)—are included in the collection, as are essays on the spirit by Kerényi, Wili, Rahner, Portmann, and others. The god Apollo in many ways acts as a symbol for the spirit within the psyche, so Kerényi's book of essays on the god may help round out this concept further by way of what James Hillman (after Henry Corbin) has called imaginal psychology: psychological understanding wrought through images and imagination.

To Begin

"The Phenomenology of the Spirit in Fairytales," cw 9, I, pp. 207–254.

"The Psychological Foundations of Belief in Spirits," cw 8, pp. 301–318.

"Spirit and Life," cw 8, pp. 319–337.

To Go Deeper

"The Spiritual Problem of Modern Man," cw 10, pp. 74–94.

"The Spirit Mercurius," cw 13, pp. 193–250.

Related Works

"On the Psychology and Pathology of So-Called Occult Phenomena," cw 1, pp. 3–88.

Secondary Sources

Campbell, Joseph, ed. *Spirit and Nature: Papers from the Eranos Yearbooks.* Princeton: Princeton University Press, 1954.

Kerényi, Karl. *Apollo.* Dallas: Spring Publications, 1983.

9. EROS AND LOGOS/
MASCULINE AND FEMININE

In explaining what for Jung were the ways and means of the psyche, rather than focusing on particular symbols or personified figures of the unconscious, we come across a pair of principles that Jung saw operating within the psyche as eternal opposites: Eros, the feminine principle of relatedness, and Logos, the masculine principle of knowledge. Obviously, as eternal principles of human behavior, Eros and Logos are not to be understood as residing exclusively in one gender or the other, literal men or women, simply because Jung identified Eros with the feminine and Logos with the masculine. For Jung, these terms, *masculine* and *feminine*, meant primarily two things.

First, *masculine* and *feminine* certainly meant what was, in Jung's time, socially defined as masculine and feminine. Thus, the feminine role of women in his time was one highly bound up with interpersonal relatedness—as wife, mother, helper—as well as tied to particular personality characteristics, such as emotionality, subtlety, aestheticism, and spirituality. These aspects of the Eros principle could, therefore, be called feminine in the sense that they constituted at that time the conventional Western definition of femininity. Similarly, the masculine role of men at that time was based on their ability to use logic and rationality in the world—as businessmen, professional achievers, providers—and consisted of related personality characteristics, such as clear thinking, activity, highmindedness,

45

problem-solving, and abstraction. In this way, Logos could be called the masculine principle, according to collective social norms. However, second and most important, Jung called these two opposite principles of human behavior masculine and feminine to indicate how such principles had been represented archetypally throughout the ages: the Eros principle of relatedness by way of female figures, such as Aphrodite (the god Eros's mother), and the Logos principle through male figures, such as Apollo and Christ.

In the time since Jung wrote, there has been a great deal of controversy concerning the validity of gender-identified sex roles, and the advent of the women's movement worldwide has succeeded in challenging these collective views of masculinity and femininity in myriad ways. What is important in reading Jung on Eros and Logos is to keep in mind that, however frequently he may have identified these principles with men and women themselves, the principles remain abstract, patterns of human behavior not intrinsically allied with anatomical gender. Indeed, certain Jungian analysts are questioning whether it is helpful to continue calling Eros feminine and Logos masculine, since both men and women share and structure their lives around both principles and, for the sake of wholeness, every individual should continue to strive for such a union of opposites. Clearly, Eros, however feminine the principle, is a mighty male god in Greek mythology, just as many representations of Logos, such as Sophia, the mystic figure of Wisdom, have had female faces.

Jung coined these terms in their psychological sense not as frames within which to fit individual men or women but rather as fluid, flexible containers for certain qualities that both women and men possess. Indeed, as one can see from the stress on individuality in his writings, Jung's intention was the very opposite of the conventional social norms, and Jung often discusses Eros and Logos precisely in order to point out how these collective images of masculinity or femininity hinder and cripple the individual through one-sidedness. Again and again, Jung insists on the importance of Eros-relatedness for men and Logos-directedness for women, having himself seen too many cases of neurotic consciousness-cramping in the service of fitting into collective gender-identified norms.

Thus, the reader might do best to read Jung on Eros and Logos in just the manner intended—lightly, tentatively, loosely, not as the final word at all, but rather as sketches toward understanding yet another pair of opposite forces within the individual soul.

A special note on Eros, however, is in order. At times throughout his career Jung used the term in a way other than to denote the principle of relatedness, specifically, as imagistic shorthand for sexuality, in line with Freud's usage of the term. The context usually makes Jung's meaning clear, since he rarely discusses Eros as a principle without also mentioning Logos and almost always specifies that it is the principle, and not the psychologized Greek god of love, to which he is referring.

The principle article in the list of readings, "Woman in Europe," is a fascinating piece on femininity and the place of women in society and social transformation, despite the dated character of many of its observations. The other material on Jung's use of Eros and Logos as psychological principles is scattered in writings on broader questions of masculinity and femininity, for instance, in his discussion of anima/animus in *Aion,* in the secton "The Personification of Opposites" in his alchemical study *Mysterium Coniunctionis* and in the brief discussion of anima/animus in "Commentary on 'The Secret of the Golden Flower.'" The fragmentary character of these references should demonstrate that Jung's thought on these psychological principles was still just in the stage of formulation.

As for secondary sources, I've resisted turning this list into a bibliography of the now enormous literature on gender. The works listed deal more or less with Jung's ideas of Eros/Logos and provide basic texts with which one should be familiar.

Jung's openness to analyzing women and training women as analysts led to the existence of a number of noted female Jungians under his direct tutelage, most of whom went on to write about the psychology of women from an archetypal perspective. M. Esther Harding's writings are classic contributions to the Jungian literature on the feminine, whereas Marion Woodman represents the next generation of Jungian thought on feminine experience quite forcefully and quite well. The only work that comes close to a monograph on Logos as the masculine principle is *Phallos: Sacred Image of the Masculine,* by Eugene Monick, though certainly a great deal of writing has been done on masculine psychology from an archetypal perspective since Jung (see the chapters "Father," "Hero," "Wise Old Man," and "Trickster" in Part Two). Robert Johnson's three books also represent enduringly popular works on these issues of Eros-femininity and Logos-masculinity, and the second of Johnson's books listed here, *She,* presents one of three important Jungian analyses of the myth of Eros and Psyche. The other two, by James Hillman in *The Myth of Analysis* and by Erich Neumann in *Amor and Psyche,* are also listed here. As representatives of contemporary reformulations of Jung's basic concepts, Tacey's and Hill's works are excellent examples of current, politically aware uses of Jung's notions.

To Begin

"Woman in Europe," CW 10, pp. 113–133.

To Go Deeper

Aion, CW 9, II, esp. chap. 3, "The Syzygy: Anima and Animus," pp. 11–22.

Mysterium Conjunctionis, CW 14, esp. chap. 3, "The Personification of the Opposites," pp. 89–258.

"Commentary on 'The Secret of the Golden Flower,' " CW 13, esp. chap. 4, "Phenomena of the Way," pp. 29–43.

Related Works

"On the Psychology of the Unconscious," CW 7, esp. chap. 2, "The Eros Theory," pp. 19–29.

"The Psychology of the Transference," CW 16, esp. chap. 1, Introduction.

Secondary Sources

Harding, M. Esther. *Women's Mysteries: Ancient and Modern.* New York: Harper & Row, 1971.

Woodman, Marion. *Addiction to Perfection: The Still Unravished Bride.* Toronto: Inner City Books, 1982.

Monick, Eugene. *Phallos: Sacred Image of the Masculine.* Toronto: Inner City Books, 1987.

Johnson, Robert A. *He.* San Francisco: Harper & Row, 1983.

Johnson, Robert A. *She.* San Francisco: Harper & Row, 1986.

Johnson, Robert A. *We.* San Francisco: Harper & Row, 1985.

Hillman, James. *The Myth of Analysis.* San Francisco: Harper & Row/Torch Books, 1983.

Neumann, Erich. *Amor and Psyche.* Princeton: Princeton University Press, 1956.

Hill, Gareth S. *Masculine and Feminine: The Natural Flow of Opposites in the Psyche.* Boston: Shambhala Publications, 1992.

Tacey, David. *Remaking Men: Jung, Spirituality and Social Change.* London: Routledge, 1997.

10. PSYCHOLOGICAL TYPES

Next to his theory of dreams and dream interpretation lies Jung's most enduring contribution to the field of psychology, his theory of psychological types. Intrigued by the conflict between Freud and Adler, in which ostensibly identical empirical data yielded such radically different theories, Jung developed a theory of psychological types that helped to shed some light on the difficulties, misunderstandings, and, of course, the natural affinities that exist in certain relationships between individuals.

According to Jung's typology, people might be classified according to attitude type and function type. Of attitude type there are two choices: extraverted, in which the individual's libido tends to be directed from himself or herself toward objects in the outer world, or introverted, in which the individual's libido tends to be directed from the objects in the outer world into himself or herself. Acknowledging that neither of these categories is fixed and exclusive, Jung sought merely to describe in a practical, observable way that someone's dominant or typical attitude was toward people, the world, and oneself.

Of function types, there are four, two categorized as rational, and two categorized as irrational. The two rational types are thinking and feeling. The term *rational* is used because both of these functions use criteria to organize and decide. The thinking function organizes and decides according to rules of analysis and logic; the feeling function organizes and decides on the basis of values and individual worth. Because feeling and emotion tend to be used synonymously these days, one must see that Jung's use of the word *feeling* includes what one might commonly term *emotion* but goes far beyond feelings to a realm of morality and values, including one's ethical sense of things and situations. Hence the appellation *rational* for feeling types in the Jungian sense might confound modern-day people (especially thinking types!) who assume feelings and emotions are always irrational aspects of psychic life meant to be controlled or resolved.

The two irrational functions, in Jung's system, are intuition and sensation. The term *irrational* is used because these function types do not *decide* primarily but rather *experience* first. The intuitive type functions primarily on the basis of his or her unconscious experience and perceptions, that immaterial realm of symbols and images of which many people are completely unaware but which an intuitive person uses as the foundation for action and experience. The sensate type functions primarily through the experience of the concrete, physical world, a down-to-earth sense of existence in the world and of oneself. To sum up, Jung postulated eight basic types of people: extraverted thinking, feeling, intuitive, and sensate, and introverted thinking, feeling, intuitive, and sensate.

Because such an empirical classification of such a psychological typology lends itself so extraordinarily well to quantitative measurement, an entire body of test instruments and related literature has grown up around Jung's relatively simple schema of personality types. The well-known Myers-Briggs test of psychological type is based on Jung's typology, though few people are aware that the test reflects Jung's typology with an extra category of "judgment/perception" added to the function types. Other Jungian analysts have developed similar tests: Joseph and Jane Wheelwright, in conjunction with Horace Gray, developed a short-form test following Jung's two-attitude, four-function typology exactly, and June Singer with Mary Loomis developed a multiaxial typology with an accompanying test released in 1984. Clearly, the theoretical usefulness of Jung's personality typology is matched by its utility on the clinical level, providing at least some organized, impersonal way of viewing human interactions which is inherently free of value judgments or prejudice.

Psychological Types, Jung's exposition of his theory and his interpretive application of it to various areas of human experience, is quite a tome by itself, and volumes have since been written amplifying the typological descriptions. *Psychological Types* was the first book Jung published subsequent to his break with Freud and as such marks Jung's reemergence into the public light of professional psychology in 1921. The long four-year period of professional isolation, his so-called fallow period, permitted Jung to develop and apply his ideas on typology to all the various aspects of culture that are the focus of each chapter of the book—philosophy, theology, poetry, mythology, psychology, and so on. In the last chapter of the book, "Definitions," Jung put forth for the first time in an organized fashion the various concepts he had come to use in the course of his work. While extraordinarily helpful and accessible, "Definitions" nevertheless is representative only of Jung's early thought, and many of the concepts defined here underwent considerable elaboration and refinement over Jung's long career. As a whole, therefore, volume 6 of the *Collected Works* represents a high point for Jung personally and professionally—a book that is the fruit of an important period of transition and self-definition as well as a lasting contribution to the field of psychology.

Reading the book is another matter, however. Chapter 10, ostensibly the last chapter in the book, is best read first, since it lays out Jung's typology in an organized fashion. Without reading chapter 10 first, one may not have much of an idea of Jung's purpose in the preceding nine chapters, in which he applies his typological constructs in great (and sometimes torturous) detail to various pairs of opposites—Plato and Aristotle, Origen and Tertullian, Schiller and Goethe, Spitteler and Goethe, the intrapsychic-aesthetic conflict of Nietzsche—to get a better grasp on the psychological foundation behind these conflicts. Jung also looks at other personality typologies proposed throughout the centuries, such as the ones put forth by Friedrich von Schiller, Furneaux Jordan, and William James, providing critiques and support in light of his own theory. These nine chapters may be approached in order, since their topics are fairly distinct from one another, or one may pick and choose, according to one's interest. The reader versed in German literature may choose the chapters on Schiller, Nietzsche, Spitteler, and Goethe, those versed in the history of the Christian church may wish to read the chapter on classical and medieval thought, and readers interested in psychology may wish to begin with the chapters on psychopathology, human character, and modern philosophy.

The secondary sources listed were chosen from the vast literature on typology because the authors explicitly deal with Jung's approach rather than focusing on other ways his typology could be used and applied.

To Begin

Psychological Types, CW 6, chap. 10, "General Description of the Types," pp. 330–407.

To Go Deeper

Psychological Types, CW 6, chaps. 1–9, pp. 3–329.

Psychological Types, CW 6, epilogue, pp. 487–495.

Psychological Types, CW 6, appendix, "Four Papers on Psychological Typology," pp. 497–555.

"On the Psychology of the Unconscious," CW 7, esp. chap. 4, "The Problem of the Attitude Type," pp. 41–63.

"The Significance of Constitution and Heredity in Psychology," cw 8, pp. 107–113.

"The Tavistock Lectures," cw 18, esp. Lecture 1 and Discussion, pp. 5–35.

"Symbols and the Interpretation of Dreams," cw 18, esp. chap. 4, "The Problem of Types in Dream Interpretation," pp. 216–226.

Related Works

Psychological Types, cw 6, chap. 11, "Definitions," pp. 408–486.

Secondary Sources

Von Franz, Marie-Louise, and Hillman, James. *Lectures on Jung's Typology.* New York: Spring Publications, 1971.

Sharp, Daryl. *Personality Types: Jung's Models of Typology.* Toronto: Inner City Books, 1987.

Spoto, Angelo. *Jung's Typology in Perspective.* Evanston, Ill.: Chiron Publication, 1995.

11. PSYCHOTHERAPY

The often erroneous characterizations of Jung and analytical psychology as abstruse, mystical, credulous, and unscientific ignore the fundamental fact that Jung undertook his many researches into psychological phenomena not as disinterested scientist but rather as practicing clinician. Jung's writings are evidence that his personality had a notably practical bent, and thus psychotherapy might well be called the cornerstone of his psychology, the purpose and motivation for his various, far-ranging researches, and his constant *point de repère,* the place to which Jung always returns. Psychology meant little to Jung if it was not useful in relieving the suffering of his patients, and he was notorious for spending little time on that which would not have a practical application.

Jung's writings on psychotherapy are therefore some of his most accessible articles for the general public, which may be the reason that volume 16, containing many of these papers, was the first of the *Collected Works* published in English. Jung's view of psychotherapy was heavily influenced by Freud's idea that true healing comes about not through the suggestion or positive influence of the therapist but rather through a dynamic resolution of unconscious conflicts, which is effected by bringing to awareness feelings, thoughts, and impulses that have been kept from awareness. Thus, Jung shares with Freud the emphasis on individual treatment, but he goes further than Freud in emphasizing the essential individuality of each patient, choosing to abandon all preconceived theoretical formulations when faced with an individual patient. This radically individual emphasis results in Jung's often discussing psycho-therapy as if it were indistinguishable from what he termed the individuation process. For this reason, both his ideas on psy-chotherapy and his concept of individuation must be under-stood for one to truly understand Jung's ideas on the nature of healing.

On the level of technique, Jung makes a distinction be-tween analytic and synthetic methods within psychotherapeutic treatment, that is, methods that reduce and explain symptoms on the basis of their regressive, childhood meanings and meth-ods that see within apparently pathological symptoms the pros-pects of future constructive growth. He sees the analytic relationship as the crux of therapy, but he differs with Freud in his evaluation of the transference/countertransference rela-tionship. For Jung, psychotherapy, the healing of the soul, oc-curs as much through resolution of the transference as through the true relationship between analyst and patient, the relationship of mutual commitment and care that occurs be-tween healer and healed. Jung places great emphasis on dream interpretation and includes within his technical armamentar-ium nonverbal methods of approaching unconscious contents, such as art, fantasy, and active imagination. Jung makes a dis-tinction between the purpose of psychotherapy for those in the first half of their lives, who have yet to build their outward lives and acquire a coherent, individual personality, and those who seek psychotherapy in the second half of life, as he calls it, for whom outer achievement no longer has quite the importance it once had and whose psychological task is now an inward jour-ney toward individual fulfillment.

Jung's equal valuation of conscious and unconscious and his practical, down-to-earth, "whatever works" attitude toward psychotherapy stand in marked contrast to the two major streams of psychological thought within the United States, be-haviorism and Freudian psychoanalysis, with their overweening emphasis on technique and their respective overvaluations of conscious and unconscious contents. Jung's writings on psychotherapy, many of which are directed to nonpsychologists, are refreshing glimpses into how he sees the healing process and his place within it. Since Jung's life work was precisely this, his work as a healer, the importance of his views on psychotherapy cannot be overestimated theoretically or personally.

The articles from volume 16 are grouped in the list that follows according to accessibility, pertinence, and depth of treatment, with the first articles listed being the easiest understood, while the subsequent articles develop his ideas on psychotherapy further. Under "Related Works" are listed reports of Jung's treatment of patients which give some sense of Jung's therapeutic technique. Under "Secondary Sources," *Jungian Psychotherapy*, by Michael Fordham, is written mainly for practicing clinicians, *Boundaries of the Soul*, by June Singer, is what one might call the standard and most popular account of Jungian analysis, and *Jungian Analysis*, edited by Murray Stein, is a unique collection of papers on Jungian psychotherapy from a variety of perspectives and on a variety of subjects. Recent contributions concerning technique by Kast, Kugler, Bradway, and McCoard round out this list.

To Begin

"What Is Psychotherapy?" cw 16, pp. 21–28.

"Some Aspects of Modern Psychotherapy," cw 16, pp. 29–35.

"The Aims of Psychotherapy," cw 16, pp. 36–52.

"Principles of Practical Psychotherapy," cw 16, pp. 3–20.

"The Realities of Practical Psychotherapy," cw 16, pp. 327–338.

To Go Deeper

"The Problems of Modern Psychotherapy," cw 16, pp. 53–75.

"Psychotherapy and a Philosophy of Life," cw 16, pp. 76–83.

"Medicine and Psychotherapy," cw 16, pp. 84–93.

"Psychotherapy Today," cw 16, pp. 94–110.

"Fundamental Questions of Psychotherapy," cw 16, pp. 111–125.

"The State of Psychotherapy Today," cw 10, pp. 157–173.

Related Works

"Psychic Conflicts in a Child," cw 17, pp. 3–35.

"A Study in the Process of Individuation," cw 9, I, pp. 290–354.

"The Tavistock Lectures," cw 18, esp. Lecture 5 and Discussion, pp. 135–182.

"The Theory of Psychoanalysis," cw 4, esp. chap. 9, "A Case of Neurosis in a Child," pp. 204–226.

"The Relations Between the Ego and the Unconscious," cw 7, pp. 123–241.

Secondary Sources

Forham, Michael. *Jungian Psychotherapy.* New York: Wiley, 1978.

Singer, June. *Boundaries of the Soul.* New York: Doubleday, 1972.

Stein, Murray, ed. *Jungian Analysis.* Boulder: Shambhala, 1984.

Kast, Verena. *The Dynamics of Symbols: Fundamentals of Jungian Psychotherapy.* Translated by Susan A. Schwartz. New York: Fromm, 1992.

Kugler, Paul, ed. *Jungian Perspectives on Clinical Supervision.* Zurich: Daimon, 1995.

Bradway, Kay, and McCoard, Barbara. *Sandplay: The Silent Workshop of the Psyche.* London: Routledge, 1997.

12. TRANSFERENCE/ COUNTERTRANSFERENCE

Jung's idea of transference within the analytic relationship was similar to Freud's, with several important differences based on Jung's ideas about the psyche. While Jung agreed with Freud that the phenomenon of transference consisted of thoughts, feelings, and fantasies from another relationship, usually in the past, being reexperienced within a present relationship, Jung differed from Freud in seeing that a transference may not be based solely on material from the personal unconscious but may contain striking archetypal elements as well. One may have a father transference to an analyst that goes beyond anything the patient ever experienced with his or her own father, experiencing the analyst as a larger-than-life, perhaps even mythically idealized figure, an experience most appropriately called an archetypal transference.

Though both Freud and Jung shared the view that transference was an ever present element of every relationship, Freud viewed transference and its analytic counterpart, countertransference, as a largely pathological occurrence between people— inappropriate, irrational, lacking reality orientation. For this reason, Freud saw transference within the analytic relationship as a matter for constant, focused exploration between analyst and patient until, ideally, the whole of the transference had been made conscious, worked through, and ultimately resolved.

Jung, however, viewing the psyche as a naturally occurring phenomenon, removed transference/countertransference from the realm of psychopathology, seeing it as a natural occurrence, perhaps unavoidable and at times even helpful. For these reasons, he differed sharply with psychoanalysis, holding the view that the real relationship between analyst and patient was potentially much more curative than the transference relationship and that the lack of transference was actually a positive factor in the analytic relationship. Further, Jung saw the transference of personal or archetypal material onto the person of the analyst as something primarily to be tolerated but certainly not promoted, something to be understood but not necessarily resolved. Within Jungian analysis, therefore, the transference and countertransference relationship is often acknowledged and explored without becoming the sole focus of treatment. Indeed, as one can see in light of Jung's theory of the collective unconscious, resolution of the transference would mean making conscious the vast ocean of collective human experience—a manifest impossibility. Jung worked to make conscious the wholeness that the unconscious transference/countertransference relationship represents, thereby hoping to bring into awareness the deep levels of existence that the patient experiences and reexperiences within the analytic relationship.

To explicate his transformational view of the transference/countertransference relationship within analysis, Jung used the symbolism of the alchemical process, a process of changing base metals into gold which the alchemists of the Middle Ages believed to be literally possible but which Jung saw as a projection of an inner, psychic process onto external, material reality. The point of the analytic process, for Jung, was to change the base metals of unexamined, projected experience into the gold of a more unified, personally integrated experience, not simply to resolve the transference on the level of the personal unconscious. Jung's definitive and highly influential study of alchemical symbolism as it pertains to transference within analysis, "The Psychology of the Transference," in its pictorial and symbolic richness could not be more unlike typically Freudian psychoanalytic treatments of the topic.

Among Jungian analysts, a wide range of opinion exists on the place of transference/countertransference in analysis. Some analysts make transference analysis the centerpiece of analytic work, particularly the so-called London School of Jungian analysts following Michael Fordham's lead, while others follow Jung's own opinions more closely and relativize the place of transference analysis in psychotherapy. The secondary sources in the readings list show the variation in how transference is conceived of and handled therapeutically by contemporary analysts.

The readings list begins with Jung's ideas on transference during his period of association with Freudian psychoanalysis, followed by an article that gives Jung's more typical view of transference. Jung's most important work, "The Psychology of the Transference," is suggested under "To Go Deeper," since the reader may wish to become more acquainted with Jung's psychological studies of alchemy before delving into this unusual piece of Jung's writing.

To Begin

   "Some Crucial Points in Psychoanalysis," CW 4, pp. 252–289.
   "The Theory of Psychoanalysis," CW 4, esp. chap. 8, "Therapeutic Principles of Psychoanalysis," pp. 181–203.
   "The Problems of Modern Psychotherapy," CW 16, pp. 53–75.

To Go Deeper

   "The Psychology of the Transference," CW 16, pp. 164–323.

Related Works

Elsewhere in this book, see the readings lists in chapter 28, "Coniunctio," and in part 4, "Esoterica."

Secondary Sources

Fordham, Michael. *Jungian Psychotherapy*. New York: Wiley, 1978.

Jacoby, Mario. *The Analytic Encounter: Transference and Human Relationship*. Toronto: Inner City Books, 1984.

13. INDIVIDUATION

Because the collective unconscious represents the source of psychic growth, Jung believed that a working relationship between the conscious and the unconscious levels of existence was vital to psychic health. This working relationship between unconscious and conscious levels of existence was also conceived and described by Jung as the relationship between the individual ego complex and the archetype of the Self, an archetype of wholeness and completion represented by symbols that Jung continually came across in the dreams and fantasies of his patients. When the conscious and unconscious, ego and Self, have an ongoing relationship, Jung saw that one could then hold together a sense of one's unique individuality as well as one's connection to the larger experience of human existence, enabling one to live in a truly creative, symbolic, and individual way.

The process of coming into this psychic balance Jung termed *individuation,* a principle and a process that he understood as underlying all psychic activity. The tendency of the psyche to move toward wholeness and balance is a fundamental postulate of Jung's psychology. Variously termed teleological, purposive, synthetic, constructive, or final, the principle that the psyche tends toward wholeness also contains the typically Jungian postulate that real human life consists of opposites that need to be united within the human soul. The process and result of such a union of opposites is the ability to form for oneself a unified, coherent, and yet unique individual personality of depth and richness. Individuation, this process of becoming one's own individual, may be understood from its etymology, that is, the process of becoming indivisible, or at one with oneself.

One purpose of analysis, perhaps *the* purpose of analysis, in Jung's view is to aid the individuation process, particularly on the archetypal level. Jung saw individuation in the way he used the term as largely a matter of psychological development in the second half of life, that is, after one's external achievements in youth and young adulthood had grown less important. Though certainly many things may occur within analysis that may not be strictly centered upon facilitating individuation in the Jungian sense—for example, problem solving or simple empathic understanding—the highest goal of analysis nevertheless is a furthering of the patient's individuation process through the exploration and experience of the archetypal symbols and figures in dreams, visions, active imagination, and everyday life.

The short articles indicated under "To Begin" are concise expositions of Jung's ideas on the subject. His accounts of the individuation processes of his patients, their individual journeys toward wholeness, are among the most engrossing stories within the *Collected Works,* in particular the one extended account he provided in "A Study in the Process of Individuation." Also indicated is that section of "Transformation Symbolism in the Mass" wherein Jung draws parallels between the rituals of the Mass and the symbolic action of the Self in the individuation process.

Given the centrality of this concept to Jungian analysis, it is not surprising that a number of analysts have written on the individuation processes they have assisted in their clinical work. While Jolande Jacobi's book gives a more theoretical treatment of the concept, Wheelwright and Adler, as older Jungian authors, with Carotenuto and Bosnak writing from a more contemporary and creative standpoint, all provide up-close looks at just how Jung understood this process to be enacted in psychotherapy.

To Begin

"Adaptation, Individuation and Collectivity," cw 18, pp. 449–454.

"Conscious, Unconscious and Individuation," cw 9, I, pp. 275–289.

To Go Deeper

"A Study in the Process of Individuation," cw 9, I, pp. 290–354.

"Concerning Mandala Symbolism," cw 9, I, pp. 355–384.

"Transformation Symbolism in the Mass," cw 11, esp. part 4, "The Psychology of the Mass," pp. 247–296.

Related Works

"The Undiscovered Self," cw 10, pp. 247–305.

Secondary Sources

Jacobi, Jolande. *The Way of Individuation*. New York: New American Library, 1967.

Adler, Gerhard. *The Living Symbol: A Case Study in the Process of Individuation*. New York: Pantheon, 1961.

Wheelwright, Jane Hollister. *The Death of a Woman*. New York: St. Martin's Press, 1981.

Carotenuto, Aldo. *The Vertical Labyrinth: Individuation in Jungian Psychology*. Toronto: Inner City Books, 1981.

Bosnak, Robert. *Dreaming with an AIDS Patient*. Boston: Shambhala Publications, 1989. Reissued by Delta in 1997 as *Christopher's Dreams: Dreaming and Living with AIDS*.

14. RELIGION

Because Jung did not live his intellectual life in reaction to Freud, comparisons between them are usually helpful only in the historical sense and not in the psychological or theoretical sense. However, when the subject is religion, the difference between the two men's psychological outlook is as edifying as it is great, explaining to a large degree why Jung's ideas may be finding more and more of a home in a modern world whose faith in rationality has been shaken in so many ways.

With regard to religion, Freud did not move much beyond his concepts of repression and sublimation, seeing incestuous Oedipal desires repressed and transformed in the various religious systems practiced by people throughout the world. Religion, therefore, is a kind of defensive fantasy re-creation of the family situation, in the form of gods, in order to subjugate unacceptable longings and impulses into a more acceptable form. The oxymoronic title of Freud's work on religion, *The Future of an Illusion*, states quite succinctly his view of religion as an illusory result of repression and sublimation, which may be useful in the creation of civilization and yet fantastic and irrational, as he implies, an illusion without a future.

Jung, on the other hand, noted several pertinent facts with regard to religion. First, there is no civilization, present or past, on the planet that has not had a religion, a set of beliefs and sacred rituals. Thus, Jung posited that there exists a religious instinct within human beings, an inherent striving toward a relationship with a Something or a Someone that transcends human limitations, a higher power.

Second, in Jung's eyes, the irrationality of religious beliefs does not reduce their inherent value as irrefutable psychic facts. Jung noted the overwhelming importance of religious beliefs to individuals and entire societies, an importance depreciated and underestimated when these are dismissed as irrational or illusory. Refraining from the near-religious faith modern people have in salvation through the power of rational thinking and technology, Jung acknowledged that much of human experience was indeed irrational, ineffable, and symbolic. Jung believed psychology as a discipline could be capable of working rationally and scientifically with basically irrational data, *only if* these data, religion in this case, were not dismissed reductively but taken altogether seriously.

Third, Jung's broader and more sophisticated knowledge of mythological systems, religious practices, and comparative ethnology led him to see that by no means did Western religious beliefs, ancient or modern, constitute the whole of world religions. Though many elements of many religions might be interpreted as projections of personal family conflicts onto the heavens in a kind of cosmic transference, Jung's wide-ranging familiarity with world religions showed him that by no means was that all there was to religious beliefs, Eastern or Western.

Because Jung did not dismiss religion but took it as a psychic fact of undeniable importance in individual and collective existence, he has been accused of being a mystic, a cloud-gathering spinner of fantasy, an unscientific dreamer. The reality is that Jung consistently dealt with religion as a psychologist and disavowed both a wish and an ability to prove the empirical truth of any religious belief. As his writings confirm, he was neither a theologian nor a metaphysician, and he examined the symbolic and psychological importance of religious experience in great depth without making any statements as to the objective truth or falsehood of any religious belief. His concern, first and foremost, was psychological, and his interest in religion derived primarily from his psychological desire to understand the often mysterious workings of the soul in greater depth, not from a desire to find God or to prove the objective existence of transcendent reality.

Jung's observation of the universality of religion led him to view religion as a manifestation of the collective unconscious. In this regard, he noted that religion actually referred to two distinct things. First, religion was religious experience, the direct contact with the divine, that which he called the *numinosum* (a term he borrowed from Rudolph Otto), manifested in dreams, visions, mystical experiences. Second, religion consisted of religious practice, the doctrines and dogmas as well as the rituals and enactments, which Jung saw as necessary to protect people from the awesome power of such a direct experience of the numinous. Both religious experience and religious practice were, therefore, for Jung psychological phenomena that found their source inwardly and outwardly in the collective unconscious. Thus, to separate Jung's discussion of specifically religious symbolism from his discussions of other types of symbols is difficult, since all manifestations of the collective unconscious are in a certain sense religious, objects of devoted attention that demand respect.

By separating religion from institutional churches and creeds, by seeing religion more as an attitude than as a set of beliefs, and by understanding religion as a psychological phenomenon of the first order, Jung's writings on religion might in a certain sense have more of an effect on modern individuals who have "lost faith" than on those who have found and practice a set of religious beliefs. Though often criticized and misunderstood, Jung's attitude toward religion and his investigations into the psychology of religion are among his most brilliant contributions to modern thought and redeem religion for modern people as an aspect of human existence at once both vital to human fulfillment and amenable to investigation and understanding.

Jung's writings on religion, as one can see from the list that follows, were extensive and ranged from technical to more popularly oriented discussions. While the more popular articles were aimed at helping the general public see how psychology and religion were not inimical but had many important points of contact, Jung's more technical explorations of theological and religious imagery in the West are among his most famous (some would say infamous) achievements. For example, "Answer to Job," in which Jung grapples with the problem of good and evil biblically and psychologically, as well as his psychological interpretation of Roman Catholic ritual and theology in "Transformation Symbolism in the Mass," are famous for the controversy they provoked. Much of Jung's writing on Eastern religion is concerned both with the psychological exploration of these symbols and with a differentiation between Eastern and Western modes of thought and experience. It is clear from these pieces that Jung intended to offer a critique of those Europeans who believed that rejecting their own Western cultural and religious heritage and unthinkingly adopting Eastern religious beliefs and practices would automatically resolve their religious questions and unrest.

Jung's ideas on religion, especially Christianity, have deeply influenced many Jungian analysts from religious backgrounds as well as many pastoral counselors working in denominational settings. Among Jungians, no one has delved into the relationship between Jung's psychology and Christianity more systematically and over a longer period of time than Edward Edinger, and so two of his many books are listed here. John Dourley's *The Illness That We Are* and Kluger's collection of writings from a Jewish perspective are included to give a sense of the contemporary scene. But the list cannot be complete without including the anthology series published by New Falcon and edited by J. Marvin Spiegelman, which systematically examine the major world religions from a Jungian angle.

To Begin

"Psychology and Religion," CW 11, pp. 5–105.

"Foreword to White's *God and the Unconscious,*" CW 11, pp. 299–310.

"Psychotherapists or the Clergy," CW 11, pp. 327–347.

"Psychoanalysis and the Cure of Souls," CW 11, pp. 348–354.

"The Undiscovered Self," CW 10, pp. 247–305.

"The Psychology of Eastern Meditation," CW 11, pp. 558–575.

"Yoga and the West," CW 11, pp. 529–537.

"Foreword to Suzuki's *Introduction to Zen Buddhism,*" CW 11, pp. 538–575.

To Go Deeper

"A Psychological Approach to the Dogma of the Trinity," CW 11, pp. 107–200.

"Transformation Symbolism in the Mass," CW 11, pp. 201–296.

"Answer to Job," CW 11, pp. 355–470.

"Psychological Commentary on *The Tibetan Book of the Great Liberation,*" CW 11, pp. 475–508.

"Psychological Commentary on *The Tibetan Book of the Dead,*" CW 11, pp. 509–526.

"Commentary on *The Secret of the Golden Flower,*" CW 13, pp. 1–56.

"Foreword to the *I Ching,*" CW 11, pp. 589–608.

Related Works

Aion: Researches into the Phenomenology of the Self, CW 9, II.

"The Undiscovered Self," CW 10, pp. 247–305.

Secondary Sources

Edinger, Edward F. *Ego and Archetype: Individuation and the Religious Function of the Psyche.* Baltimore: Penguin Books, 1972. Boston: Shambhala Publications, 1992.

Edinger, Edward F. *The Christian Archetype: A Jungian Commentary on the Life of Christ.* Toronto: Inner City Books, 1987.

Dourley, John. *The Illness That We Are.* Toronto: Inner City Books, 1984.

Kluger, Rivkah. *Psyche in Scripture: The Idea of the Chosen People and Other Essays.* Toronto: Inner City Books, 1995.

Spiegelman, J. Marvin, ed. *Sufism, Islam and Jungian Psychology.* Tempe, Ariz.: New Falcon Publications, 1991.

Spiegelman, J. Marvin, ed. *Judaism and Jungian Psychology.* Tempe, Ariz.: New Falcon Publications, 1993.

Spiegelman, J. Marvin, ed. *Hinduism and Jungian Psychology.* Tempe, Ariz.: New Falcon Publications, 1987.

Spiegelman, J. Marvin, ed. *Buddhism and Jungian Psychology.* Tempe, Ariz.: New Falcon Publications, 1995.

Spiegelman, J. Marvin, ed. *Catholicism and Jungian Psychology.* Tempe, Ariz.: New Falcon Publications, 1995.

Spiegelman, J. Marvin, ed. *Protestantism and Jungian Psychology.* Tempe, Ariz.: New Falcon Publications, 1996.

15. SYNCHRONICITY

Synchronicity, since Jung's introduction of the concept in 1951, has remained among the most original and controversial ideas in analytical psychology and, at times, one of the most difficult to grasp. The title of Jung's work on the subject, *Synchronicity: An Acausal Connecting Principle*, provides the term's definition: Synchronicity is a principle that links events acausally, that is, in terms of the subjective meaningfulness of the coincidence, rather than by cause and effect. Thus, understanding synchronicity and synchronistic events requires a way of thinking almost entirely foreign to Western culture, a way of thinking that does not separate the physical world from interior psychic events. The phrase that often occurs with regard to Jung's concept of synchronicity is *unus mundus*, Latin for "one world." Synchronicity requires that one consider the world a unified field in which subject and object are fundamentally one, two different manifestations of the same basic reality.

A common misunderstanding of this concept, and therefore a common but erroneous criticism, is that synchronicity is equivalent to a principle of magic agency, that the outer occurrences experienced as meaningful coincidences were *caused* somehow by the inward, contemporaneous psychic processes. The error lies in confusing what Jung insists is an *acausal* connecting principle with the typical Western *causal* connection. If I am thinking at a particular moment of an individual and then, significantly and uncannily, he happens to telephone, to call this coincidence synchronistic is not to say that my thoughts were the cause of the phone call. To term this coinci-

dence synchronistic, in the way Jung defines the concept, is to
see the coincidence as a potentially important indication of a
psychological connection in its meaning to me. The connection within a synchronistic event is subjective, on the level of
the personal, emotional meaning of the coincidence when an
inner state meets an outer occurrence in an especially powerful
and transformative way.

Jung noted that the numinous quality of synchronistic
events was derived from the fact that "the emotional factor
plays an important role" in these occurrences and that "meaningful coincidences—which are to be distinguished from
meaningless chance groupings—therefore seem to rest on an
archetypal foundation." The quality of feeling that accompan-
ies synchronistic events is perhaps the most striking characteristic of such events. According to Jung, the feeling quality
produced by a synchronistic event and the psychic energy that
it evokes find their source in that stratum of psychic interconnections which Jung called the collective unconscious.

Synchronicity: An Acausal Connecting Principle is readily accessible to a general readership, unlike many other works by
Jung. Chapter 2, "An Astrological Experiment," is especially
interesting, however, and may need an introductory comment.
Jung takes the horoscopes of 180 married couples and does a
statistical analysis to see whether or not traditional astrological
assumptions concerning the planetary conjunctions of married
people is actually borne out by the data at a level of significance
greater than chance. What Jung finds is that the traditional
astrological assumptions do in fact occur at an astonishing fre-
quency in the sample, but from this he concludes not that a
causal factor is at work, but rather that *his own* excitement and
interest in the project influenced the results in a way that co-
incided with traditional astrological ideas. Thus, without a care-
ful reading, one might assume (as many have done, in error)
that Jung is attempting a pseudoscientific proof of astrology,

whereas Jung actually uses this experiment to show one's own emotional interest can even seem to influence supposedly scientific data in a way that supports one's own unconscious expectations.

The articles listed under "To Go Deeper" are there not because of their difficulty—in fact, they are quite easy to read—but rather because they give a fuller sense of Jung's views on synchronicity. The first is a short lecture on synchronicity given at the Eranos conference of 1951, which preceded publication of Jung's larger work. The second is Jung's well-known introduction to the translation of the *I Ching* by his friend Richard Wilhelm, in which Jung explores the synchronistic uses to which this Chinese book of wisdom has traditionally been put and reports the results of his own throwing of the I Ching. The last two readings are short pieces from volume 18, the collection of miscellaneous writings not included in other volumes of the *Collected Works*.

Since there will probably never be an end to the discussion of synchronicity, which has blossomed into prominence lately with a spate of books taking the concept in all sorts of directions, the secondary sources listed hew closely to Jung's own ideas and approach.

To Begin

   Synchronicity: An Acausal Connecting Principle, cw 8, pp. 417–519.

To Go Deeper

   "On Synchronicity," cw 8, pp. 520–531.
   "Foreword to the *I Ching*," cw 11, pp. 589–608.
   "An Astrological Experiment," cw 18, pp. 494–501.
   "Letters on Synchronicity," cw 18, pp. 502–509.

Related Works

   Elsewhere in this book, see the readings list in chapter 33, "Occult Phenomena."

Secondary Sources

Bolen, Jean Shinoda. *The Tao of Psychology: Synchronicity and the Self.* San Francisco: Harper & Row, 1979.

Von Franz, Marie-Louise. *On Divination and Synchronicity: The Psychology of Meaningful Chance.* Toronto: Inner City Books, 1980.

Aziz, Robert. *C. G. Jung's Psychology of Religion and Synchronicity.* Albany: State University of New York Press, 1990.

Hopcke, Robert H. *There Are No Accidents: Synchronicity and the Stories of Our Lives.* New York: Riverhead, 1997.

PART TWO

ARCHETYPAL FIGURES

16. EGO

Before looking at particular archetypes, one is obligated to mention Jung's concept of the ego complex, sometimes referred to by Jung as the self (with a lowercase *s*), ego consciousness, or simply ego. Since the Freudian usage of the term has become the most common, denoting a psychic structure that mediates societal demands (the superego) and instinctual drives (the id), one might assume, incorrectly, that Jung's usage of the concept is the same or similar. For Jung, the ego is a complex, a feeling-toned group of representations of oneself that has both conscious and unconscious aspects and is at the same time personal and collective. Simply put, too simply perhaps, the ego is how one sees oneself, along with the conscious and unconscious feelings that accompany that view.

Jung never dismisses the importance of the ego in human development; after all, the ego represents the very hard-won self-awareness that makes us human. He consistently points out, however, that the ego is one of many complexes within the psyche and, at times, one that stands on shaky ground. As compared to the agelessness of other archetypal dominants within the psyche, the ego of modern humanity is a relative newcomer on the scene and so is prone to being swamped, so to speak, by other, more powerfully charged complexes. In the most benign of such cases, the result of the ego's being overwhelmed may be the simple exclamation, "Gee, I wasn't myself last night! What came over me?" In the worst instance, the result may be psychosis, neurosis, or mass hysteria on a grand scale. Therefore, Jung's view of ego is one that radically relativ-

izes our self-awareness and sense of cosmic importance, showing our "selves" to be residing in a psychic universe that is
larger than our own fragile, fleeting self-image and conscious
awareness.

Since this ego complex is hardly the be-all and end-all of
human existence, but rather a group of self-representations
which is highly important at some times and only relatively important at others, Jung had many psychological objections to
the modern idealization of the ego or the individual self. His
writings point out how the ego, if it is to carry consciousness,
must do so with *complete* consciousness, recognizing its human
limitations and the unconscious factors, positive and negative,
that affect it.

For this reason, Jung extensively explored the relationship
between the ego and what he termed the Self, the archetype of
wholeness within the collective unconscious. If our ego has lost
contact with the Self, unsettling feelings of alienation arise
within—a meaninglessness, perhaps depression, the sense of
being adrift, without direction or hope—feelings that seem so
frequently to characterize contemporary lives. On the other
hand, if our ego has become too closely connected to the Self,
arrogating to ourselves the endless possibilities and dynamic
power of this larger psychic Self, the result is what Jung termed
inflation, a sense of exhibitionistic grandiosity, an unrealistic
view of oneself as omnipotent, omniscient, unassailable. This is
the ego of those well-known cultural figures, the egomaniac
and the egotist.

All of this should make clear why in the *Collected Works* Jung
consistently discusses the ego in relation to other aspects of the
psyche. One is never really given an extended monographic
treatment of the ego but rather a more comprehensive, relativ-
ized picture of how the ego fits into the bigger picture. In the
readings list, under "To Begin," are included the definition of
ego Jung gives at the end of *Psychological Types* and the short

section on the ego which Jung wrote prefacing his larger study of the Self, *Aion*. "On the Nature of the Psyche" gives a good overview of Jung's conception of the ego and its relationship to consciousness and unconsciousness, as does the short article "Child Development and Education," which indicates how Jung thought of the ego's development and emergence within an individual child.

"To Go Deeper" lists Jung's most extended treatment of the ego. "The Relations between the Ego and the Unconscious," which is contained in volume 7 of the *Collected Works, Two Essays on Analytical Psychology,* a volume which represents an important theoretical touchstone for Jung's psychology. Also indicated, for those whose interest waxes scholarly, is the appendix to "The Relations between the Ego and the Unconscious," entitled "The Structure of the Unconscious," which reveals preliminary thoughts on topics Jung developed further elsewhere. Because the archetype of the Hero is so often a symbol of ego consciousness emerging from the matrix of the primordial unconscious, the "Related Works" list includes Jung's most extended treatment of this material, part 2 of *Symbols of Transformation.*

As for secondary sources, Edward Edinger's classic book *Ego and Archetype* is an excellent treatment of the place of ego within Jungian psychology. Likewise, Neumann's somewhat formidable volume *The Origins and History of Consciousness* is concerned with how ego consciousness emerges from the unconscious, how it develops and through what stages, and how this psychic process has been represented mythologically throughout the ages.

To Begin

>*Psychological Types,* cw 6, esp. chap. 11, "Definitions," under "Ego," p. 425.

Aion, CW 9, II, esp. chap. 1, "The Ego," pp. 3–7.

"On the Nature of the Psyche," CW 8, pp. 159–234.

"Child Development and Education," CW 17, pp. 49–62.

To Go Deeper

"The Relations Between the Ego and the Unconscious," CW 7, pp. 123–241.

"The Structure of the Unconscious," CW 7, pp. 269–304.

Related Works

Symbols of Transformation, CW 5, esp. part 2, pp. 121–444.

Secondary Sources

Edinger, Edward F. *Ego and Archetype: Individuation and the Religious Function of the Psyche.* Baltimore: Penguin Books, 1972. Boston: Shambhala Publications, 1992.

Neumann, Erich. *The Origins and History of Consciousness.* Princeton: Princeton University Press, 1954.

17. SHADOW

Using images from the material world to describe psychic facts is often the unfortunate but necessary lot of psychologists, as the object of their study will always be nonmaterial, psychic, beyond simple matter. In the case of the shadow, this metaphorical necessity becomes a virtue, for one can understand Jung's concept of the shadow best by taking the physical metaphor very seriously. Just as any bright light must always cast darkness somewhere, the conscious brightness of the ego always casts a shadow in one's personality, a shadow with the same relationship to the ego's power and potentialities as a photographic negative has to the actual photograph.

Those unpleasant and immoral aspects of our selves which we would like to pretend do not exist or have no effect on our lives—our inferiorities, our unacceptable impulses, our shameful actions and wishes—this shadowy side of our personality is difficult and painful to admit. It contradicts who we would like to see ourselves as, who we would like to seem to be in the eyes of others. Our egoistic sense of self, our autonomy, our uprightness, senses its authority challenged by this shadow and feels the shadow's closeness as a threat, a dark brother/sister continually at our heels, awkward, nettling, anxiety-provoking, shameful.

For this reason, Jung noted how this shadow and all its qualities often fall into unconsciousness or may even be actively, ruthlessly suppressed to maintain the sanctimonious sweetness of our illusory perfection. Unconsciousness, however, does not rob the shadow of its existence or its power, just as ignoring our physical shadow does not prevent its shading whomever or whatever falls in its path. Indeed, Jung saw how this psychic shadow, when repressed or denied, continues to work behind the scenes, causing all manner of neurotic and compulsive behavior. Jung also noted that, instead of repressing or denying the shadow, we may also project the shadow onto others, attributing to other people those nasty, unsavory qualities that we would like to deny in ourselves. Shadow projection can thus result in paranoia, suspiciousness, and a lack of intimacy, all of which afflict individuals, groups, even entire nations. Far from solving the problem, shadow projections act only to exacerbate the troublesome quality of this dark side of our soul, injecting a kind of poison into interpersonal relationships through self-righteous denial and distorted perceptions.

Jung upheld the psychic necessity of recognizing the shadow within, however embarrassing or distressing, acknowledging its unpleasant qualities and its offensive behavior, coming to terms with its mischief and mayhem, owning its character as ours and no one else's. His accounts of psychotherapy demonstrate how the individuation process almost always begins with this humbling integration of the shadow into one's conscious sense of self, the first and most important task on the road to psychic health. To bring the shadow to consciousness depotentiates it, as Jung would say, deprives it of its power, since consciousness-raising drags all the shadow's long-hidden impulses and fantasies into the realm of moral choice, so that one faces the often difficult ethical decisions and the distasteful self-discipline sometimes avoided through neurosis.

Jung considered the shadow an aspect of the collective unconscious, since everyone's ego casts a corresponding shadow within the psyche, but he also acknowledged that the character of an individual's shadow is highly influenced by personal and cultural factors. While the shadow's close relationship to the ego may facilitate its integration into consciousness, true knowledge of the shadow is a task never really completed. As an archetypal figure, the shadow is not actually a problem to be solved but rather an inner entity to be explored, known, and recognized as a part of our psychic and communal lives.

The other sense of the shadow which appears in Jung's writings, especially in his discussions on religion and Christianity, is related to the shadow of the individual psyche but goes considerably beyond this to what is best called the objective shadow, the shadow as the archetype of darkness itself, the absolute evil that, Jung posits, must exist in the collective unconscious as the only logical counterpart to the shining light of absolute good. This objective shadow, this darkness cast by the brightness of God as the Self, is what Jung sees denied, repressed, and projected by the doctrine of Christian theology, and Jung's tireless argument with the dogmatic exclusion of the objective shadow from Christianity runs through much of his works. His plea that the Devil be accepted as a reality, his vision that only such a dark and diabolic Fourth could truly provide for the wholeness missing in the Christian Trinity of Goodness in Three Faces, his attraction to the many noncanonical writings concerning the place of the objective shadow of evil in the universe—all these earned him a reputation for being Gnostic, a thinker for whom the duality of good and evil seemed a better representation of the actual psychic condition of humanity than did the Christian conception of life and soul. This shadow as archetype *an sich,* the archetype as such, is Jung's second, larger, and perhaps more revolutionary idea of the shadow, the foundation on which one's individual shadow stands, the "dark side of the Force" that we meet again and again on the world stage of the twentieth century.

The readings listed here cover all these aspects of Jung's exploration of the shadow, beginning with its psychological definition and its place in the unconscious life of the individual, then going further into Jung's major writings on the place of the shadow in the horrors of World War II and in the context of Christianity. Since the Trickster figure within the psyche often functions as shadow carrier, Jung's article on the Trickster is noted under "Related Works." Marie-Louise von Franz's excellent series of seminar presentations on the shadow individually and in fairy tales represents how Jung's followers conceived of and used the concept of the shadow in analytical psychology. Because an individual's inferior function, according to Jung's theory of personality types, often carries the shadow, as analytical psychologists are wont to say, von Franz's lecture "The Inferior Function," in *Jung's Trilogy,* serves to enrich one's understanding of the shadow in everyday life. More contemporary work on this topic is represented by the books by Brinton-Perera and Sanford, and the lively mixture of Jungians and others in the anthology *Meeting the Shadow.*

To Begin

Aion, cw 9, II, esp. chap. 2, pp. 8–10.

"Archetypes of the Collective Unconscious," cw 9, I, pp. 3–41.

"The Problems of Modern Psychotherapy," cw 16, pp. 53–75.

To Go Deeper

"After the Catastrophe," cw 10, pp. 194–217.

"The Fight with the Shadow," cw 10, pp. 218–226.

"Epilogue to 'Essays on Contemporary Events,' " cw 10, pp. 227–243.

Answer to Job, cw 11, pp. 357–470.

Related Works

"On the Psychology of the Trickster Figure," cw 9, I, pp. 255–272.

Secondary Sources

Von Franz, Marie-Louise. *Shadow and Evil in Fairy Tales.* Dallas: Spring Publications. Boston: Shambhala Publications, 1995.

Von Franz, Marie-Louise. "The Inferior Function." In von Franz, Marie-Louise, and Hillman, James. *Jung's Typology*. New York: Spring Publications, 1971.

Brinton-Perera, Sylvia. *The Scapegoat Complex: Toward a Mythology of Shadow and Guilt*. Toronto: Inner City Books, 1986.

Sanford, John A. *Evil: The Shadow Side of Reality*. New York: Crossroad Press, 1987.

Zweig, Connie, and Abrams, Jeremy, eds. *Meeting the Shadow*. New York: Tarcher, 1991.

18. PERSONA

All of human life is not lived in the depths. As vital as the movements of the unconscious are to human existence, conscious awareness and the quality of day-to-day living will never be displaced as legitimate and necessary components of human wholeness. Despite all his depth psychology, much of Jung's approach and many of his concepts are not at all mystical or far-fetched. As an aspect of the personal and collective psyche, the persona may be counted among Jung's less abstruse and more practical conceptions. From the Latin word for an actor's mask, which in turn represents his role within the play, the persona, in the psychological meaning coined by Jung, is that part of the personality developed and used in our interactions, our conscious outer face, our social mask. Our persona may be a well-developed, socially adapted face—the famous writer, the devoted spouse, the rising young executive—or, on the contrary, a well-developed but socially unadapted face—the rebellious artist, the argumentative gadfly, the stubborn curmudgeon—but it is still the persona, a face and a role shown to others and used to give form to our outward sense of self.

Many of Jung's comments on the persona have the quality of looking down on the persona as an inferior or uninteresting segment of the psyche, and this derogatory view of the persona seems based largely on Jung's personal psychology, especially his introversion and the inward focus of his psychology, especially his introversion and the inward focus of his psychological researches. Also clear from his writings on persona is that, as an analyst, Jung encountered many people who had, to their detriment, identified with their personas to the neglect of their inner lives, believing themselves to be nothing more than their social position or external professional accomplishments. This persona identification, as Jung called it, was not infrequently the cause of the very psychological troubles that had brought the patient to the doorstep of his consulting room. Thus, one might have the sense from reading Jung (as well as many of his followers) that the persona is something undesirable, something to be shattered or removed, a false self.

In actuality, for all his negative evaluations, Jung acknowledge the importance of the persona, however superficial its psychological nature. Jung saw that the persona functions as mediator between the outer world and the ego, a mediator comparable in importance to the anima/animus, which serves as mediator between the ego and the unconscious. For this reason, Jung considered the persona as a collective segment of the psyche, since the persona takes its form and function from its relationship to outward, collective reality. Far from shattering the persona, Jung saw the persona as a vital sector of the personality which provides the individual with a container, a protective covering for his or her inner self.

Because of this protective function, issues concerning one's persona often appear in dreams in situations or events involving clothing and makeup: we find ourselves trying on innumerable hats in a closet filled with gorgeous gowns; we find ourselves walking naked down a city street on the way to an exam; we walk into an important business meeting without our pants. Like our outer clothes and makeup, the persona may be overdone and insubstantial, a way of pretending to be someone we aren't, or it may be underdone and inadequate, leaving us exposed and vulnerable. In the best case, the persona is appropriate and tasteful, a true reflection of our inner individuality and our outward sense of self. Therefore, the persona is like many of the archetypal figures we meet in the *Collected Works,* with both positive and negative aspects, helpful at times and hindering at others.

The readings on this topic reveal that the persona has not received a great deal of sustained attention. Jung's definition of persona from chapter 11 of *Psychological Types* appears within his discussion of psyche, and similarly, Jung discusses persona at most length in "The Relations between the Ego and the Unconscious," one of his *Two Essays in Analytical Psychology*. As for secondary sources, the fact remains that the only full-length book on the topic in English by a first-generation analyst is Jolande Jacobi's *Masks of the Soul,* which does not concentrate that exculsively on persona itself, despite its evocative title. My own book is an attempt to show how relevant the persona and its vicissitudes can be personally, socially, and collectively.

To Begin

Psychological Types, cw 6, esp. chap. 11, "Definitions," under "Soul [Psyche, personality, persona, anima]," pp. 463–470.

To Go Deeper

"The Relations Between the Ego and the Unconsious," cw 7, pp. 123–241.
"The Structure of the Unconsious," cw 7, pp. 269–304.

Secondary Sources

Jacobi, Jolande. *Masks of the Soul.* Grand Rapids, Mich.: William B. Eerdmans, 1976.
Hopcke, Robert H. *Persona: Where Sacred Meets Profane.* Boston: Shambhala Publications, 1995.

19. ANIMA/ANIMUS

Jung's discovery of the anima/animus as an archetype of the collective unconscious remains one of his unique contributions to human knowledge and certainly one of his most creative. From his clinical work, his experiences within his own family, and his own self-explorations, Jung observed that beneath his conscious masculine personality there seemed to lie an unconscious feminine side with its own particular character and its own particular ways of acting. Indeed, Jung saw that this softer, warmer, more emotional and spiritual side beneath a man's conscious masculinity had a kind of autonomy and coherence that rendered it not unlike an inner woman, especially since in dreams, fantasies, and projections, this side of his masculinity actually took the symbolic form of a woman. Likewise, as Jung relates in his autobiography, *Memories, Dreams, Reflections,* he observed in his mother (and subsequently in other women as well) two personalities: The first was a normal, everyday feminine personality, while the second was a more mysterious but very real personality that seemed to resemble an unconscious masculine side to her conscious femininity, a side with traits and modes of behavior generally ascribed to men, such as ruthlessness, rationality, power, and a kind of stalwart, opinionated quality quite at odds with her normal motherly self-presentation.

Because these sub-personalities existed on the unconscious level and in Jung's experience seemed universally present, Jung believed them to be archetypes of the collective unconscious. He called the man's feminine counterpart the anima, the Latin word for soul, and the woman's masculine counterpart the animus, or masculine soul. Taken together, therefore, Jung called this pair contrasexual archetypes to denote how the anima and animus are symbolic modes of perception and behavior which are represented by figures of the opposite sex within an individual's psyche. Because unconscious, the femininity or masculinity represented by the anima or the animus, Jung noted, was generally ill developed, and for this reason, Jung sometimes referred to the anima as a man's inferior femininity and to the animus as a woman's inferior masculinity, using the word *inferior* in the double sense of lying beneath one's conscious personality and functioning imperfectly.

Despite this double-sided inferiority, these contrasexual archetypes appeared to Jung to have the role of guide to the unconscious, a mediator/mediatrix between one's ego and one's inner life, inviting and leading one into a deeper understanding of one's unconscious world. Evidence for this mediatory function of the anima/animus Jung found in the dreams of his patients, wherein anima/animus figures regularly served as companions and helpers to the dreamer, echoing countless folktales and pieces of great literature in which a figure of the opposite sex, an Other, leads the hero or heroine to the goal at the end of the story. Further evidence concerning the anima/animus Jung found in the way that certain individuals seemed identified with these archetypes, or anima/animus-ridden—men behaving like moody, stereotypically hysterical women, women possessed by an all too stereotypical masculine spirit of ill will and hunger for power—while other individuals seemed primarily to project these inner figures onto idealized individuals of the other sex, men making their girlfriend or wives over into the image of the Madonna, women continually searching for their white knight in shining armor.

The concept of the anima/animus is, therefore, among

Jung's most important, in the sense that it affords explanations of phenomena that would be difficult to understand otherwise. If the opposite sex were, in fact, totally other and different, what would be the cause of such eternal and enduring attraction, unless the opposite sex represented something incomplete, something to be known and experienced within oneself, an inner figure that strives toward completion and relationship? Jung understood the anima/animus mainly from within the confines of the stereotyped patterns of masculinity and femininity characteristic of the early twentieth century. Since contemporary thought on masculinity and femininity has changed, expanded, and even, to some extent, become more muddled, there are similarly a variety of thoughts on and expansions of the concept of the anima/animus from subsequent Jungians: Is the anima always female, the animus always male? Does the anima always incarnate a man's Eros, the animus a woman's Logos? How do the symbolic manifestations of an archetype—especially social roles and stereotypes concerning men and women—become shaped by culture? Jung's uncovering and naming of these contrasexual archetypes raises these questions without resolving them fully, making the anima/animus perhaps one of the most evocative and well explored of all of Jung's concepts.

A special way in which Jung used the anima/animus concept, notably in his early writings, is related to the linguistic roots of the terms—anima/animus as soul image, the inward personification of one's psyche, not simply one's feminine or masculine side. This use of the term sums up quite well the importance of the anima/animus psychologically, since it ties together the diverse threads of this archetypal constellation: the soul as mediator between Self and ego, between self and other; the soul as the wellspring of true relatedness and creative power; the soul as the source of our identity and our fulfillment.

One exaggerates only slightly to say that rarely Jung wrote anything without referring to the anima or animus, and references to the anima/animus run into five pages in the general index to the *Collected Works*. The readings listed here include only those writings in which Jung turned his full attention to explication of these archetypes. Under "Related Works" are found those articles on diverse topics which treat the anima/animus fairly extensively. Three secondary sources that give a fair indication of the development of Jungian thought on the anima/animus are *Animus and Anima,* by Jung's wife, Emma Jung; the Jungian classic *Anima as Fate,* by Cornelia Brunner; and James Hillman's tour de force on the topic, *Anima: The Anatomy of a Personified Notion.* Hillman's work is actually three books in one, consisting of an extended essay on the various aspects of anima, accompanied by relevant quotations from Jung and followed by notes that serve as a bibliography. John Sanford's treatment of the anima/animus in *The Invisible Partners* may be perhaps the most down-to-earth of all secondary sources and the easiest for individuals unfamiliar with Jungian psychology to tackle, and the Ulanovs' book provides an up-to-date, though more technical, discussion of the concept.

To Begin

Aion, cw 9, II, esp. chap. 3, "The Syzygy: Anima and Animus," pp. 11–22.

Psychological Types, cw 6, esp. chap. 11, "Definitions," under "Soul [Psyche, personality, persona, anima]," pp. 463–470, and under "Soul-Image," pp. 470–472.

To Go Deeper

"The Relations Between the Ego and the Unconscious," cw 7, esp. part 2, chap. 2, "Anima and Animus," pp. 188–211.

"Concerning the Archetypes with Special Reference to the Anima Concept," cw 9, I, pp. 54–72.

"Woman in Europe," cw 10, pp. 113–133.

"Mind and Earth," cw 10, pp. 29–49.

Related Works

"Marriage as a Psychological Relationship," cw 17, pp. 189–201.

Psychology and Religion, cw 11, esp. sections 1 and 2, pp. 5–63.

"Commentary on 'The Secret of the Golden Flower,' " cw 13, esp. section 4, "Phenomena of the Way," pp. 29–43.

"Psychological Aspects of the Mother Archetype," cw 9, I, pp. 75–110.

Symbols of Transformation, cw 5, esp. part 2, chap. 7, "The Dual Mother," pp. 306–393.

"The Psychology of the Transference," cw 16, esp. section 2, "King and Queen," pp. 211–235.

Secondary Sources

Jung, Emma. *Animus and Anima.* New York: Spring Publications, 1957.

Brunner, Cornelia. *Anima as Fate.* Dallas: Spring Publications, 1986.

Hillman, James. *Anima: The Anatomy of a Personified Notion.* Dallas: Spring Publications, 1985.

Sanford, John A. *The Invisible Partners.* New York: Paulist Press, 1980.

Ulanov, Ann, and Ulanov, Barry. *Transforming Sexuality: The Archetypal World of Anima and Animus.* Boston: Shambhala Publications, 1994.

20. SELF

For Jung, the individual ego complex not only exists in relationship to other complexes of the psyche but draws its stability and growth from a larger, more complete sense of human wholeness, which Jung saw as archetypically based. This archetype of wholeness he termed the self. While the editors of the *Collected Works* do not capitalize *self*, whether referring to the archetype or simply to one's individual ego—leaving it to the context of the passage to indicate which meaning was intended—in English the convention has since developed of referring to the individual ego as the *self*, with a lowercase *s*, and the archetype as the *Self*, with a capital *S*. The capitalization of *Self* in its archetypal denotation is as much for clarity of terminology as for psychological reasons, since the Self is just that, in Jung's view: the archetype of a supraordinate, organizing principle of psychic selfhood.

Jung discovered symbols of the archetypal Self in many of the world's religious systems, and his writings stand as testimony to his continued fascination with these symbols of completion and integration: the paradisiacal past of unbroken unity symbolized by the Garden of Eden or the Golden Age of Olympus; the mythological World Egg from which all creation is said to have sprung; the hermaphroditic Original Man, or *anthropos*, who represents humanity before its fall and degradation, or the human being in its most pristine state, such as Adam, Christ, Buddha; the mandalas of Asian religious practice, those exquisitely beautiful squared circles used as the focus of meditative discipline, intended to bring one to a greater awareness of all reality. As a psychologist, rather than as a philosopher or theologian, Jung saw that this organizing archetype of wholeness was particularly well captured and developed through specifically religious imagery, and he thus came to understand that the psychological manifestation of the Self was indeed the experience of God or the "God-image within the human soul." Obviously, Jung did not intend to reduce the almighty, transcendent Divine Being to a psychological experience, a mere archetype of humanity's collective unconscious; rather, his purpose was to show how the image of God exists within the psyche and acts in suitably God-like ways, whether one's belief in God is conscious or not.

Further, Jung noticed that, if the psyche is a natural and purposive phenomenon, much of this purposiveness seemed centered on the action of the archetypal Self within. The meaningfulness of events, uncanny interventions and solutions that appear in the midst of problematic situations, synchronistic phenomena in which strange coincidences result in the transformation of previous attitudes—all of these psychic occurrences Jung put down as manifestations of the Self, in the way that such phenomena laid bare and facilitated a more all-encompassing sense of one's existence. The natural corollary to this observation is that psychological analysis helps to forge a greater connection to the Self for the individual, moderating the inflation or alienation that occurs when the individual ego is too closely identified or too out of touch with the Self and its integrative power.

The nature of the Self as the psychological image of transcendence makes much of Jung's writing on this archetype difficult to follow, since the relevant passages often occur within the context of religious imagery or in discussions of the individuation process. Jung's masterwork on Christian symbolism, *Aion,* subtitled "On the Phenomenology of the Self," is the most extensive treatment of his ideas of the Self but can be difficult to read. Under "To Begin," therefore, are listed Jung's definition of the Self from *Psychological Types,* followed by the two sections of *Aion* that do not require extensive preparation or study. To explore the topic further, one must delve into readings that do not deal with the Self directly but rather approach the subject by way of detailed examinations of symbolism drawn from religion, clinical practice, and other sources. Most surprising to a reader unfamiliar with the *Collected Works* may be Jung's exploration of unidentified flying objects (quaintly and noncommittally called "things seen in the skies") as possible symbols of wholeness from beyond our immediate experience. These readings on the Self are an example of what Jung called circumambulation, walking around a concept until its various aspects are illuminated and understood.

Among secondary sources, Edward Edinger's classic text, *Ego and Archetype,* looks at the relationship between ego and the Self theoretically; his *Encounters with the Self* examines the same ego-Self relationship by way of William Blake's illustrations of the Book of Job; and his lecture transcript *The Transformation of the God-Image,* on Jung's "Answer to Job," provides further depth in an accessible format. Mario Jacoby's *Longing for Paradise* examines the myths of paradise as Self-symbols in the maturation of collective consciousness and in the individuation process, and two essays in particular, "Cosmic Man" and "Jung's Discovery of the Self," in von Franz's collection shed light on the development of the concept in Jung's thought.

To Begin

> *Psychological Types,* cw 6, esp. chap. 11, "Definitions," under "Self," pp. 460–461.

> *Aion,* cw 9, esp. chap. 4, "The Self," pp. 23–35, and chap. 5, "Christ, a Symbol of the Self," pp. 36–71.

To Go Deeper

"The Relations between the Ego and the Unconscious," CW 7, esp. chap. 1, "The Function of the Unconscious," pp. 173–187, and chap. 4, "The Mania-Personality," pp. 227–241.

"A Study in the Process of Individuation," CW 9, I, pp. 290–354.

"Concerning Mandala Symbolism," CW 9, I, pp. 355–384.

"A Psychological Approach to the Dogma of the Trinity," CW 11, esp. chap. 4–6, pp. 148–200.

"Transformation Symbolism in the Mass," CW 11, esp. chap. 4, section 3, "The Psychology of the Mass: The Mass and the Individuation Process," pp. 273–296.

Related Works

Flying Saucers: A Modern Myth of Things Seen in the Skies, CW 10, pp. 309–433.

"The Undiscovered Self," CW 10, pp. 247–305.

Secondary Sources

Edinger, Edward F. *Ego and Archetype: Individuation and the Religious Function of the Psyche.* Baltimore: Penguin Books, 1972. Boston: Shambhala Publications, 1992.

Edinger, Edward F. *Encounter with the Self: A Jungian Commentary on William Blake's "Illustrations of the Book of Job."* Toronto: Inner City Books, 1986.

Edinger, Edward F. *The Transformation of the God-Image: An Elucidation of Jung's* Answer to Job. Toronto: Inner City Books, 1992.

Jacoby, Mario. *Longing for Paradise: Psychological Perspective on Archetype.* Boston: Sigo Press, 1980.

Von Franz, Marie-Louise. *Archetypal Dimensions of the Psyche.* Boston Shambhala Publications, 1997.

21. MOTHER

Jung spent considerable time examining and explicating the role of the Mother archetype in the psychology of the unconscious, and since his fascination with this archetypal dominant has been shared by his followers, there is a large, rich literature on the Mother archetype from a Jungian standpoint. Various things account for Jung's attention to this particular archetype. His complex relationship with his own mother, his delight in women, his singular focus on the unconscious as the matrix (from *mater*, mother) of consciousness, and the overwhelming patriarchalism of modern culture all seem to have joined forces to endow the Mother archetype with great personal and collective significance to Jung. On this score, one might even accuse him of enantiodromia, a term he used to describe a kind of psychic running back in the opposite direction, the overcompensation that regularly occurs if one's consciousness has been too rigidly one-sided for too long a time. In a culture so dominated by individual men and by masculine ideals, over which the Christian male trinity of Father, Son, and Holy Spirit has presided now for two millennia, Jung's interest in Mother and all she represents stands as a salutary corrective to the single-minded collective masculinity of Western culture.

As with all of Jung's archetypal researches, he began with the personal, the mothers of his patients, discerning within their myriad individual stories the mother complexes that had such a telling effect on his patients' lives and loves. In this regard, Jung notes that, while the anima seems to have a life and character of her own in a man's soul, she nevertheless has a

100

close relationship to this mother complex and is strongly influenced by the archetypal image of Mother, which lies beyond the individual mother complex. Because of this connection, Jung also notes that the mother, personal and archetypal, is related to but distinct from an individual's Eros, one's capacity for relatedness and intimacy.

Thus, Jung examines how men have—indeed, must have—a different relationship to the Mother archetype than do women, and he sets about to discern the various relationships that men and women seem to play out psychologically through their enmeshment with or distance from the cluster of archetypal images which is Mother within all of us. Typically for Jung, his psychological examination of this material is organized first and foremost around primordial symbols of Mother, and all her many attributes, companions, and relationships: the chthonic Earth Mothers who gave birth to the world, the Sky Mothers whose overarching containment holds and directs the world; the Fertility Goddesses who nourish the world and feed all its people; the Dark Mother Goddesses who swallow and clutch, devour and restrict.

The importance and universality of this archetype in human life makes for a wealth of imagery from many cultures, which in turn renders Jung's writings on the Mother archetype at times a daunting task to read thoroughly. Since it is from Mother that all has sprung, so, too, psychically, Mother seems to give birth to all within, in all its multiplicity and profusion. These writings, therefore, require of the reader a certain familiarity with Jung's method if he or she is to avoid getting lost amid what often seems like a flood of symbolic material. Appropriately, this task parallels the challenge Mother presents to everyone's process of individuation: how to know Mother and yet not lose oneself in the regressive womb of childhood ways and infantile wishes, how to relate to Mother in all her wealth and not sacrifice our own lives in the process, how to be nourished and fed by Mother and still maintain our autonomy and independence.

The readings listed start with the easiest and most focused of Jung's works and then move into the more difficult and detailed material on the Mother archetype from *Symbols of Transformation* and what is perhaps Jung's most challenging work, *Mysterium Coniunctionis*. This work uses alchemical symbolism to focus on the union of opposites within the human psyche, for which the royal parental pair of Rex and Regina, King and Queen, has long been a potent symbol. Jung's sections on Luna, while more on the archetypal feminine than on Mother in particular, nevertheless indicates the fullness of Jung's thought and his passionate interest in the Great Mother. The passages from volume 5 and volume 14 may require study, and the uninitiated reader may wish to consult chapter 5 of this book, "Symbol," and read part 4, "Esoterica," before delving into these works.

Because of the recent resurgence of interest in women's experience and, as a consequence, in ancient matriarchal religion, Jung's researches provide contemporary researchers and writers with a firm psychological base from which to explore what Jean Shinoda Bolen calls "the goddesses in everywoman"—the slow differentiation that has occurred in the Mother archetype over the centuries. So many Jungians have written so much on Mother that one is faced with an embarrassment of riches in picking and choosing. Erich Neumann's book *The Great Mother* is the hands-down classic in the Jungian literature on Mother, to be read and studied before all others, while M. Esther Harding's *Women's Mysteries Ancient and Modern* and *The Parental Image* give detailed attention to the Great Mother and her place in the archetypal parental pair. More contemporary writers are represented in the following list by Ann Belford Ulanov and Jean Shinoda Bolen, whose books on the feminine point to the multifaceted nature of the Mother image and its relationship to the image of Woman in general.

To Begin

"On the Psychology of the Unconscious," CW 7, esp. chap. 6–7, pp. 80–113.

Psychological Aspects of the Mother Archetype, CW 9, I, pp. 75–110.

To Go Deeper

Symbols of Transformation, CW 5, esp. part 2, pp. 121–444.

Mysterium Coniunctionis, CW 14, esp. part 3, chap. 4, "Luna," pp. 129–183, and part 4, chap. 9, "Regina," pp. 376–381.

Related Works

Aion, CW 9, II, esp. chap. 3, pp. 11–22.

"Analytical Psychology and Education," CW 17, pp. 65–132.

Secondary Sources

Neumann, Erich. *The Great Mother.* Princeton: Princeton University Press, 1955.

Harding, M. Esther. *Women's Mysteries: Ancient and Modern.* New York: Harper & Row, 1971. Boston: Shambhala Publications, 1990.

Harding, M. Esther. *The Parental Image: Its Injury and Reconstruction.* New York: Putnam, 1965.

Ulanov, Ann Belford. *The Feminine in Jungian Psychology and Christian Theology.* Evanston, Ill.: Northwestern University Press, 1971.

Bolen, Jean Shinoda. *The Goddesses in Everywoman.* San Francisco: Harper & Row, 1984.

22. FATHER

In comparison to the depth and abiding richness of Jung's focus on the Mother archetype, Jung's work on the archetype of Father seems sketchy, desultory, and even a bit superficial. Besides one short article written during Jung's psychoanalytic period and somewhat revised subsequently, Jung spent little time and energy exploring the male half of the archetypal parental pair. For this reason, much of what Jung had to say on the Father archetype is scattered among a number of articles or must be gleaned from writings on child development or alchemical imagery, writings in which Jung examines for the most part the effect of the personal father on the life of an individual, without much archetypal amplification.

For a patriarchal culture, this is a curious situation to find in the collected works of a great psychologist, and many explanations spring to mind. Freud's overweening emphasis on the father in the psychological development of the child and in psychoanalytical theory—father internalized as superego, father as God, father as Oedipal rival and head of the primal horde, Freud's own identification of himself as the father-authority of psychoanalysis—may have drawn forth from Jung a certain kind of compensatory downplaying of the father's role. Though Jung's subtle and important shift toward valuing the feminine in all her forms—Mother, Goddess, Eros, the unconscious—was and still is needed, this emphasis on the feminine leaves a hole of sorts in Jung's writings. The lack of extended attention to Father, of course, may be largely due to Jung's own personal psychology and may reflect the relative importance of his own parental complexes in his work. More useful than such speculation perhaps is to entertain the idea that the one-sidedness of patriarchal culture leads not only to ignorance of femininity in all its forms but also to a skewed and spotty knowledge of the true nature of masculinity, a one-sidedness that Jung could not escape.

To notice the relative lack of attention given to Father by Jung is obviously not to say that archetypal masculinity remained unimportant to him personally or theoretically. The masculine archetypes of the Hero and the Wise Old Man occupy a central place in Jung's thought and are obviously closely related to the Father archetype, especially its ideal, "good" side. However, Jung left the task of a full theoretical development of the role of the Father to those following him.

The readings list begins with Jung's short article "The Significance of the Father in the Destiny of the Individual," a piece from Jung's early writings which he himself acknowledges as "too simple, too naive" in his foreword to the second edition. The simplicity and naiveté of the piece resides in its fairly exclusive focus on how the personal fathers of individual patients affect their children's lives, a focus that the other articles listed continue via case discussions of child analysis. To explore the subject further, one must tackle the rather demanding writing of Jung's alchemical works, especially the dream series presented in the second part of *Psychology and Alchemy,* wherein the archetypal imagery of the Father from the dreams of an adult male analysand reveals the comings and goings of the collective Father in his many shapes and forms.

The secondary sources indicate that Jungian analysts have striven to fill the gap in Jung's own writings, and a great deal of excellent writing now exists, from a number of perspectives, which focus on Father: his chthonic, or earthy, side; his spiritual, or heavenly, side; the intersection of personal and collec-

tive experiences; and the body of myths and legends that reveal
Father in all his potency, power, and diversity.

To Begin

> "The Significance of the Father in the Destiny of the Individual,"
> CW 4, pp. 301–323.
>
> "Psychic Conflicts in a Child," CW 17, pp. 3–35.
>
> "Analytical Psychology and Education," CW 17, pp. 65–132.
>
> *The Theory of Psychoanalysis,* CW 4, esp. chap. 9, "A Case of Neurosis
> in a Child," pp. 204–226.

To Go Deeper

> *Psychology and Alchemy,* CW 12, esp. part 2, "Individual Dream Sym-
> bolism in Relation to Alchemy: The Study of Unconscious
> Processes at Work in Dreams," pp. 41–223.

Related Works

> Elsewhere in this book, see the readings lists in chapter 25,
> "Hero," chapter 26, "Wise Old Man," and chapter 27,
> "Trickster."

Secondary Sources

> Samuels, Andrew, ed. *The Father: Contemporary Jungian Perspectives.*
> New York: New York University Press, 1988.
>
> Perry, John Weir. *Lord of the Four Quarters: Myths of the Royal Father.*
> New York: Braziller, 1966.
>
> Colman, Arthur, and Colman, Libby. *Earth Father, Sky Father: The
> Changing Concept of Fathering.* Englewood Cliffs, N.J.: Prentice-
> Hall, 1981. (reprinted as *The Father: Mythology and Changing
> Roles.* Chicago: Chiron, 1988.)
>
> Monick, Eugene. *Phallos: Sacred Image of the Masculine.* Toronto:
> Inner City Books, 1987.

23. PUER/DIVINE CHILD

The archetype of the Divine Child, the *puer aeternus,* the child within all of us, is a figure on which much attention has been lavished by Jung's followers, while Jung himself wrote little on the archtype. Quite typically, however, the little he wrote became a fertile starting point for the many subsequent treatments and descriptions of the multifaceted, baby-faced *puer.*

Jung came to the *puer* (and the *puer's* sister, the Kore, or Maiden) by way of Greek and Roman mythology, and in particular through the work of Karl Kerenyi, with whose writings Jung's own brief psychological elaborations of the archetypal figure were published. Aspects of the *puer* in mythology, as Jung sees it, closely parallel the psychological meaning that this figure has for the individual soul in dreams and inner experiences. For example, the Divine Child is a symbol of future hopes, the seedling, the potentiality of life, newness himself: Baby Jesus in Luke's nativity story springs to mind, the tiny savior of the world who is worshiped by kings and whose birth is heralded by the star and by angels from on high. However, the *puer* is more than mere child. He is also divine and so represents in some ways the forerunner of the hero, the small child that is often superhuman or possessed of astounding gifts at a tender age. Hercules' youthful feats of strength are illustrations of this connection between the *puer* and the figure of the heroic demigod. Frivolity, pleasure, and play also characterize this Eternal Child, whose archetypal character means that he will never grow up. James Barrie's Peter Pan is a modern representation of this aspect of the *puer,* just as Pan, especially in his pastoral, piping, and pleasure-bent moments, or Eros, son of Aphrodite and the beautiful, youthful god of love and pleasure, might be the best classical representations of *puer.*

These manifold qualities of the *puer,* centered on the futurity of human life and on the enlivening, charming, and refreshing elements of human experience, ensure for him a place of high regard in the pantheon of archtypal figures, and the appearance of the *puer* in the dreams and fantasies of modern individuals is for this reason invariably important. Yet all archetypes have both a light and a dark side, and the *puer aeternus* is no exception. Though Jung himself may not have developed this line of thought as elaborately as those who came after him, the phenomenon of *puer* identification, an individual whose dominant sense of self is unconsciously based on the Divine Child, is an archtypal dynamic of great import and often equally great disturbance. Enshrined in pop psychology by Richard Kiley as the Peter Pan Complex, a *puer* identification may lead to a superficially entrancing but basically immature child-man who is incapable of commitment or generativity, a flighty Little Prince with unrealistic hopes and inappropriate dreams. In this sense, the *puer* has a close connection to the archetypal Mother, for unless a man finds the right balance of dependence on and autonomy from Mother, an identification with the Divine Child, Mama's darling, may seem an attractive way out of adult responsibilities and the pain of separation.

Jung wrote only one paper on the *puer aeternus,* "The Psychology of the Child Archetype." He dealt with the emergent hero-child and his relationship to the Great Mother in certain sections of *Symbols of Transformation* which amplify his short monograph of the Divine Child. The secondary sources listed here are the two most enduring Jungian works on the *puer,* Marie-Louise von Franz's lectures transcribed and gathered in the volume *Puer Aeternus,* and the collection of articles, *Puer Papers,* which is led off by James Hillman's essay "Senex and

Puer." Also recommended is Karl Kerényi's "The Primordial Child in Primordial Times," the companion essay to Jung's work on the Divine Child archetype.

To Begin

"The Psychology of the Child Archetype," CW 9, I, pp. 151–181.

To Go Deeper

Symbols of Transformation, CW 5, esp. chap. 4. "The Origin of the Hero," pp. 171–206, and chap. 5, "Symbols of the Mother and of Rebirth," pp. 207–273.

Related Works

"Psychological Aspects of the Mother Archetype," CW 9, I, pp. 75–110.

"The Psychological Aspects of the Kore," CW 9, I, pp. 182–203.

Secondary Sources

Von Franz, Marie-Louise. *Puer Aeternus.* 2d ed. Santa Monica, Calif.: Sigo Press, 1981.

Hillman, James, et al. *Puer Papers.* Dallas: Spring Publications, 1979.

Kerényi, Karl. "The Primordial Child in Primordial Times." In Kerényi, Karl, and Jung. C. G. *Essays on a Science of Mythology.* Princeton: Princeton University Press, 1963.

24. KORE/THE MAIDEN

The collective unconscious, as Jung frequently points out, does not obey the rules and regulations of consciousness. Unlike the world of which we are aware, well ordered in space and time, the realm of the unconscious is a messy place where things transform easily, where time and space are not respected (indeed, do not exist), and where, as a consequence, it is often difficult to discriminate neatly and cleanly between one archetypal figure and another. Such is the character of Jung's work on the archetype of the Kore, associated closely with his work on the Divine Child and equally seminal.

The figure Jung examines in his major work on the subject represents many things, and the complexity of this archetype is reflected in the multiple associations of her name. Literally the Maiden, Kore is also the name for Persephone of Greek mythology, Demeter's daughter, Hades' forced bride, and the focal figure in the Eleusinian mysteries. This multiplicity of her roles in Greek mythology—virgin, daughter, bride, and queen of the underworld—is mirrored in the multiplicity of ways Jung sees this figure from his archetypal perspective. She is the companion to the *puer*, his feminine counterpart, the *puella aeterna*, as subsequent writers have dubbed her, and as such she shares with the *puer* all his playfulness, his potentialities, his heroism-to-be; she is Persephone in her springtime charm. Jung also sees in her the archetypal figure of the anima, not simply out of a desire to further his own theoretical agenda, but rather based on the mythological literature itself. As queen of the underworld, Hades' wife, she is the mediatrix between conscious and unconscious, between light and dark. As the daughter of the Great Earth Mother, she is connected to the bounty of the Self and is the agent of the soul's fulfillment; she is Persephone as the agent of the seasonal cycle of death and rebirth. She obviously represents the archetypal force of the feminine in many ways, especially the feminine in its transformative and mediatory aspects, and so, in Jung's understanding, the Kore is an archetypal figure that holds great meaning for the modern psyche, especially in the context of a civilization so maiden-hating in so many ways. Thus, in writing of the Maiden, Jung uses material from active imagination to illustrate how in many ways the feminine mysteries still exist within the souls of contemporary people and find their best symbolic expression in this many-sided figure, the Kore.

There is a single article on the archetype of the Maiden in the *Collected Works*. Under "Related Works," Jung's article on the Mother archetype is listed, because it amplifies the "Daughter" archetype in a logical and evocative way. The secondary sources listed are led off by Kerényi's works, followed by Sylvia Brinton-Perera's contemporary examination of this archetype using the Sumerian myth of the maiden-goddess Inanna-Ishtar, and Wilkinson's quite fascinating use of this myth to make a point about the psychology of victimization.

To Begin

"The Psychological Aspects of the Kore," CW 9, I, pp. 182–203.

Related Works

"Psychological Aspects of the Mother Archetype," CW 9, I, pp. 75–110.

Secondary Sources

Kerényi, Karl. "Kore." In Kerényi, Karl, and Jung, C. G. *Essays on a Science of Mythology*. Princeton: Princeton University Press, 1963.

Kerényi, Karl. *Eleusis: Archetypal Image of Mother and Daughter.* Princeton: Princeton University Press, 1967.

Brinton-Perera, Sylvia. *Descent to the Goddess: A Way of Initiation for Women.* Toronto: Inner City Books, 1981.

Wilkinson, Tanya. *Persephone Returns: Victims, Heroes and the Journey from the Underworld.* Berkeley, Calif.: Pagemill Press, 1996.

25. HERO

The great storehouse of world mythology was the source of Jung's insights into the collective unconscious and proof of his hypotheses, since mythologems—those common themes that run through the legends and folktales of the most diverse cultures—were seen by Jung as clues to enduring aspects of the psyche. One such universally present figure in mythology, regardless of the culture or the period, is the figure of the hero, a figure so central to the legends of nearly every culture that it sometimes seems almost as if heroic legends are the very definition of mythology.

While the hero figure's universality is certainly interesting sociologically and anthropologically, Jung inquired, as always, into the psychological import of this ubiquitous figure on the stage of the world's imagination. In examining various heroic legends, therefore, Jung came across identical elements in the hero's story: his divine birth; his *nekyia,* or descent into the underworld; the heroic actions he must undertake, such as battles with dreaded monsters or dangerous tasks to be performed; the presence of helpful companions, sometimes male, sometimes female, sometimes theriomorphic (i.e. animal in form); the motif of defeat, death, and rebirth.

Jung saw within these common themes that the Hero could be understood as an archetype within the collective psyche and, moreover, that this archetype was the one most often identified with humanity's slowly emerging ego consciousness. The historical appearance of human consciousness, our awareness of being aware, has a touch of the divine to it, a magical "something from nothing" with great, transformative effect, all of which comes to be reflected in the hero figure's supernatural parentage and his unusual birth. To become aware of the realm of shadowy darkness, the region of unconsciousness that lies beneath the bright sense we have of our selves, is like the hero's descent into the underworld, an unavoidable task fraught with danger, which must be accomplished in order to grow and prosper as individuals. To maintain our integrity and self-awareness is frequently a battle against long odds, involving hard work that seems to require the cleverness, help, luck, and perseverance of a figure larger than life. Due to our human limitations, this battle for awareness of self and others, conscious and unconscious, often runs in cycles that parallel the cyclical defeat and renewal depicted in heroic legends.

However important ego consciousness and however well symbolized by the archetypal Hero, Jung nevertheless was amply aware of the lethal effect of any identification that occurs when ego meets archetype: the psychic inflation of consciousness that is the result of contact with the transpersonal sphere of the collective unconscious. Though many of Jung's ideas concerning the hero have been developed much more extensively by his followers, especially Erich Neumann and Joseph Campbell, Jung's deep appreciation for the power and potentiality of the unconscious led him to be suspicious of any overvaluation of heroic ego consciousness, viewing humanity's capacity and struggle for self-awareness as but one stage in the evolution of collective consciousness, a stage perhaps now at an end and in need of transformation. For Jung, the classical Greek concept of hubris, overweening pride, applies as much to our contemporary faith in our ability to produce, act, and achieve as it did at the time of Sophocles or Homer. To identify ourselves with the Hero is to flirt with disaster, psychologically and these days even literally.

Furthermore, Jung saw that the Hero, as one manifestation of the archetypal masculine, need not always be a symbol of ego consciousness. For women, the animus, or unconscious masculine side, often fits the archetypal mold of a heroic figure struggling toward consciousness and effectiveness, a struggle with every bit of the storm and stress of so many myths. Similarly, for men, the Hero need not only symbolize awareness or achievement but also may signify a separation from Mother, that hard-won autonomy which may be a heroic, lifetime task and from which true relationship to another may emerge.

Jung's most extended presentation of the Hero archetype is in *Symbols of Transformation*. Since nearly all of part 2 of this work is devoted to tracing the personal and collective development of the hero as a symbol of libido, it is recommended under "To Begin," though it may take a good deal of thought and study to assimilate. Under "To Go Deeper" are listed writings that amplify the archetypal symbol of the Hero and Jung's concept of the mana-personality, along with dream analyses and his discussions of the hero figure in the dreams of black Americans, whom he saw as having a closer relationship to a "primitive mentality" than white Americans. Discussions of general psychological dynamics that illuminate the position of the Hero in the psyche of modern individuals are listed under "Related Works."

Neumann's *The Origins and History of Consciousness* and Joseph Campbell's *The Hero with a Thousand Faces* are the two classics on the archetype of the Hero and its many manifestations. Emma Jung's *The Grail Legend* (finished and edited by Marie-Louise von Franz after Mrs. Jung's death) is a minor masterpiece in the study of a heroic figure of European legend, Perceval/Parsifal, and Allan Chinen uses fairy tales to examine the relationship between Hero and Trickster, reformulating and updating both notions for a contemporary audience.

To Begin

> *Symbols of Transformation,* CW 5, part 2, chap. 4, "The Origin of the Hero," pp. 171–206, chap. 5, "Symbols of the Mother and Rebirth," pp. 207–273, and chap. 6, "The Battle for Deliverance from the Mother," pp. 274–305.

To Go Deeper

> "The Relations between The Ego and The Unconscious," CW 7, esp. chap. 3, "The Technique and Differentiation between the Ego and the Figures of the Unconscious," pp. 212–226, and chap. 4, "The Mana-Personality, pp. 227–241.
>
> "Mind and Earth," CW 10, pp. 29–49.
>
> "The Travistock Lectures," CW 18, esp. lecture 2, pp. 36–56, and lecture 3, pp. 70–94.

Related Works

> "Conscious, Unconscious and Individuation," CW 9, I, pp. 275–289.
>
> "The Development of Personality," CW 17, pp. 167–186.

Secondary Sources

> Neumann, Erich. *The Origins and History of Consciousness.* Princeton: Princeton University Press, 1954.
>
> Campbell, Joseph. *The Hero with a Thousand Faces.* Princeton: Princeton University Press, 1968.
>
> Jung, Emma, and von Franz, Marie-Louise. *The Grail Legend.* 2d ed. Boston: Sigo Press, 1980.
>
> Chinen, Allan B. *Beyond the Hero: Classic Stories of Men in Search of Soul.* Los Angeles: Tarcher, 1993.

26. WISE OLD MAN

"Knowledge, reflection, insight, wisdom, cleverness and intuition," Jung writes of the qualities associated with the archetypal figure he came to call the Wise Old Man. As another face of the archetypal masculine, a face quite distinct from the face of the Hero or the Father, the Wise Old Man is a universal figure in the rich body of world religion and mythology, a figure with whom Jung had direct inner contact in various forms throughout his life.

The words just quoted make clear how the archetypal Wise Old Man is the psychic personification of what Jung identified as spirit, especially spirit as knowledge or wisdom, Logos in all its many forms and effects. Though fatherly and heroic in certain ways, the Wise Old Man is also symbolic of a certain quality of masculine spirit unrelated to Father or Hero—a quietness, a hermitlike secretiveness, a force expressed not in the phallic thrustings of the Hero or in the procreativity of the Father but a force that comes from within, a magical strength that guides and fortifies one in one's inner struggles. One figure in Western culture which Jung mentions in connection with this archetype and which incarnates the Wise Old Man in popular imagination is that of Merlin in the Arthurian legends—the Wizard and Magician, the Counselor and the Guide, Old Man of the Forest and Seeker after Truth.

Like the Hero, the Wise Old Man is not a figure restricted to men's psychology alone but may appear for a woman as the incarnation of a certain side of her animus, especially that which Jung came to call the positive animus, the helpful, hidden strength of her inner wisdom and spirit, he who transforms and creates, a figure that urges onward and upward without pushing, that directs and counsels without ordering or commanding. Therefore, given the lack of any extended work by Jung on the archetype of the Father per se within the *Collected Works*, one might see the Wise Old Man, for women and for men, as a particular derivative of the archetypal Father, Yahweh in his best raiment.

Though the Wise Old Man certainly is not all there is to the Father or to masculinity on the collective level, it is to Jung's credit that his experiences with this most helpful and inspiring archetypal dominant occupy an important place within his writings. Indeed, the figure of Jung himself, particularly in his later years, came to incarnate more and more the Wise Old Man for those around him, with the result that the figure of Jung himself has gathered to it both the dark and the light sides of this archetype—Jung the ideal healer, mystic, and teacher as seen by his followers, patients, and students; Jung the founder of a cult, the pompous guru, the totalitarian sympathizer, as seen by his detractors. Thus, it is not hard to discern the Wise Old Man projection that is behind much of the recent controversies concerning Jung the person.

Jung's most extended treatment of the Wise Old Man is "The Phenomenology of the Spirit in Fairytales," whose psychological analyses of particular fairytales can be a bit complex, especially toward the end. The reader is enjoined to take some time and persevere. To delve deeper into the Wise Old Man requires going a bit further afield. Jung's well-known interest in alchemy and the works of various alchemists led him to an intimate knowledge of his Swiss compatriot, the medieval alchemist Paracelsus, a figure resembling the Wise Old Man in certain ways: eccentric, obsessed with inner wisdom, reclusive and wizardly. Jung was invited to make two short addresses for commemorative celebrations of Paracelsus which delineate

Paracelsus as a figure rather than present Paracelsus's alchemical and spiritual system (as Jung does elsewhere in great detail). The article "Concerning Rebirth" presents a figure from Islamic mysticism, Khidr, who also bears a certain resemblance to the Wise Old Man. Finally, I recommend the last chapter of *Aion,* in which Jung integrates into a single coherent structure the relationship of various archetypal figures to one another in constituting the wholeness of the Self. The Wise Old Man appears here in various forms in the quaternios Jung examines. The obvious connection of the Wise Old Man to the archetypes of both the Father and the Trickster makes it important for one to read materials on these archetypes to shed more light on the various aspects of the Wise Old Man.

A dearth of secondary sources exists on the Wise Old Man per se. Emma Jung and Marie-Louise von Franz's book, *The Grail Legend,* examines the figure and function of Merlin in the Arthurian cycle in a way that may be helpful in augmenting one's vision of this important archetypal dominant, as does the interpretation of fairytales in which Wise Old Men play a part, presented by von Franz in *Individuation in Fairy Tales.* All the same, there is a hole of sorts in the literature of the Wise Old Man, to be filled by future Jungian writers.

To Begin

"The Phenomenology of the Spirit in Fairytales," cw 9, I, pp. 207–254.

To Go Deeper

"Paracelsus," cw 15, pp. 3–12.

"Paracelsus the Physician," cw 15, pp. 13–30.

"Concerning Rebirth," cw 9, I, pp. 111-147.

Aion, cw 9, II, esp. chap. 14, "The Structure and Dynamics of the Self," pp. 222–265.

Related Works

Elsewhere in this book, see the readings lists in chapter 22, "Father," and chapter 27, "Trickster."

Secondary Sources

Jung, Emma, and von Franz, Marie-Louise. *The Grail Legend,* 2d ed. Boston: Sigo Press, 1980.

Von Franz, Marie-Louise. *Individuation in Fairy Tales.* Dallas: Spring Publications, 1980. Boston: Shambhala Publications, 1990.

27. TRICKSTER

Jung's relationship to mythologist and researcher Karl Kerényi influenced Jung's thought in many crucial ways, and some of Jung's most important essays on the psychology of archetypal figures appeared initially in tandem volumes with Kerényi's mythological studies of these figures. Just as Mother, Kore, and Divine Child were given psychological life by Jung, so to speak, through the midwifery of Kerényi, so, too, the Trickster of American Indian, Greek, and medieval alchemical mythology lives within the *Collected Works* because of the collaboration of these two men.

Those interested in logical and linear thought often find Jung's method of exposition confusing and anxiety-provoking, because archetypal patterns of the psyche are not to be grasped through straight-and-narrow argumentation but rather through an impressionistic gathering of aspects and themes until a figure emerges with a particular shape and a particular function. In such a characteristic fashion Jung approaches the Trickster, he who turns the tables on the high and mighty, the Joke-player, the source of reversals and consequently the source of transformation and change. Associated with thievery, with upsets, with foolishness and inanity of every hue, the Trickster of American Indian mythology has its archetypal counterpart in Hermes of Greek mythology, the thief, the sweet talker, the fleet-of-foot. This mythological association of Hermes as trickster, Jung found, was not lost on medieval alchemists, whose inward and outward search for transformation led them to prize the figure Mercurius as Quick-Silver, the shape-shifter, the very source of metamorphosis, an association enshrined in the term for the alchemical writings as a whole, the *corpus hermeticum.*

All archetypes have two sides, and the Trickster is no exception. In examining this archetype, another archetype of masculinity, Jung cannot help but see this archetypal Fool in many of the ways Yahweh is depicted in the Old Testament: capricious, powerful, capable of taking many forms, incomprehensible in his whims and ways. Also, Jung notices that the shadow may have much in common with the psychology of the Trickster in the way its existence continually upsets the balance of ego-dominated consciousness, giving the lie to our conscious intentions, playing painful pranks on our lofty self-importance, and thereby providing the impetus for transformation and change. Tarot decks and ordinary playing cards both preserve the figure of the Trickster in the card of the Fool or the Joker, the wild card of human existence, who can play any role, high to low, with the power to reverse and change the direction of our journey. Thus, this figure is greeted with delight and anxiety, powerful when on our side, baffling when not, an untrustworthy but altogether necessary part of our humanity.

Jung's writings on the Trickster in the *Collected Works* number but two: "On the Psychology of the Trickster-Figure" and "The Spirit Mercurius." Each of these articles is short but full of rich connections to Jung's other researches and to the other archetypal figures that cluster about the Trickster figure. Because of the way Jung ties together the shadow, the Trickster, Yahweh, Job, and Satan archetypally, "Answer to Job" provides an interesting amplification of the Trickster image by way of Jung's psychological treatment of the problem of evil in the Old Testament.

Monographs on the Trickster within the Jungian literature are hard to come by. Though much attention has been devoted to Hermes/Mercurius and though Hermes and the Trickster have much in common, the figures are not identical. Nevertheless, an excellent and classic study is Kerényi's *Hermes, Guide of Souls*. Chinen's book looks at the concept through the lens of current thought on men's issues; and I have included two wonderful collections of Native American legends concerning Coyote, the Native American trickster figure, for sheer pleasure.

To Begin

"On the Psychology of the Trickster-Figure," CW 9, I, pp. 255–272.

To Go Deeper

"The Spirit Mercurius," CW 13, pp. 193–250.

Related Works

"Answer to Job," CW 11, pp. 365–470.

Secondary Sources

Kerényi, Karl. *Hermes, Guide of Souls*. Dallas: Spring Publications, 1987.

Chinen, Allan B. *Beyond the Hero: Classic Stories of Men in Search of Soul*. Los Angeles: Tarcher, 1993.

Malokti, Ekkehart, and Lomatuway'ma, Michael. *Hopi Coyote Tales: Istututwutsi*. Lincoln: University of Nebraska Press, 1984.

Haile, Fr. Bernard. *Navajo Coyote Tales: The Curly Tó Aheedlíni Version*. Lincoln: University of Nebraska Press, 1984.

28. CONIUNCTIO

The image of the *cuniunctio*—Latin for "unification" or "union"—is one that Jung drew from alchemical writings of the Middle Ages, and so this image might best be understood through a full understanding of Jung's research into alchemical imagery. While the popular image of alchemists is that of misguided visionaries searching for ways to turn lead into gold, a chimeric pursuit long since discounted by our more rational age, Jung studied the many surviving alchemical texts to find quite a different reality: namely, that the literal pursuit of substance transformation among the alchemists was only one part of a much more sophisticated philosophical-psychological system of thought, which considered the alchemist's own personal transformation the critical factor in the success of the alchemical enterprise. Thus, Jung saw alchemical descriptions of literal, physicochemical procedures as external projections onto matter of inward psychic processes whose actual aim went beyond the transformation of base matter into gold, and whose real purpose was the spiritual transformation of the alchemist from within.

Of the many stages in certain alchemical procedures, one of the final stages was the *coniunctio oppositorum*, or the union of opposites, in which separated materials with opposite qualities were at last united to create a wholly new, transformed substance—the ultimate goal of alchemical procedures. While this *coniunctio* seems straightforward enough when described in words, the symbolism of the *coniunctio* from alchemical drawings and images is actually what impressed Jung most, for, to his great surprise, this chemical *coniunctio* was symbolized again and again by images of sexual union (including incestuous sexual union, such as the marriage of royal brother and sister) and by the half-man, half-woman figure of the hermaphrodite. To find such monstrous and shocking sexual symbolism for the end point of what was, after all, supposed to be a mere chemical operation made clear to Jung that the alchemist's *coniunctio* was much more, in fact a true symbol, as Jung understood it: an image pointing to something beyond itself, a mystery that might never be fully known.

What does the *coniunctio* point to or represent? Jung suggests that the *coniunctio,* the union of male and female found both in the royal incest imagery and in the image of the hermaphrodite, points to an inward union of male and female elements necessary for psychological and spiritual wholeness. Such a union would lead to a capacity for true intimacy and relationship, and in this regard Jung found the *coniunctio* an apt symbol for the meeting of souls that occurs between analyst and patient in the course of analysis. Obviously, given Jung's understanding of the Self, the *coniunctio* is one symbol of the psychic wholeness that the Self represents, and the divinity of the androgyne and the regal character of the incestuous lovers within the *coniunctio* of the alchemists point to a higher plane of psychological integration, which issues from the Self as archetype of wholeness.

In spite of Jung's masterful and often dense explications of the alchemical figure, the *coniunctio* remains, as in the title of volume 14, a *mysterium,* a mysterious intertwining of archetypal opposites into a final divine state of integration. While Jung wrote much concerning the male/female character of the union, the fact remains that even this may be taken less literally and more figuratively, understanding male and female as symbols of any archetypal opposites: active/passive, conscious/ unconscious, light/dark, destructive/constructive, analytic/

synthetic. Since all archetypal dominants are polarities and possess double faces, the *coniunctio,* however sexual its symbolism, represents the union of *any* opposite qualities whose reconciliation leads to greater oneness with oneself and others. The importance of the *coniunctio,* in Jung's thinking and in Jungian thought, cannot be overemphasized, however, espeically with regard to individuation and the process of analysis, where it stands as a guiding image and evocative challenge to each individual concerned with inward resolution and outward relatedness.

Jung expounds at length on this image in one of his best known and most influential papers, "On the Psychology of the Transference," which, however, is not the easiest piece of the *Collected Works* to tackle without some introduction to Jung and alchemy. The uninitiated reader may wish to consult part 4 of this book, "Esoterica," before delving into Jung's article. The thrust of "On the Psychology of the Transference" is to illustrate the process of analysis between analyst and patient by using alchemical imagery. As the goal of analysis is wholeness, Jung applies the *coniunctio* of the alchemists and the steps in its attainment to the transference/countertransference relationship and the transformation that occurs in analysis. One may imagine how this conceptualization of transference and countertransference so typical of Jung's later writings was received within the psychological community dominated by Freudian thinking on transference, countertransference, and the goal of analysis. For this reason, "On the Psychology of the Transference" must be read and studied by those who care to understand Jung's therapeutics thoroughly.

To learn more about Jung's writings on the *coniunctio* requires reading his final book, *Mysterium Coniunctionis.* While I have provided a separate introduction to this difficult but enormously rewarding masterpiece of Jung's career in part 4, those sections in *Mysterium Coniunctionis* that detail the *coniunctio* itself are noted in the following list. Under "Related Works" one finds two pieces that deal with the psyche's ability to reconcile or transcend the conflictual oppositions inherent in all of us and to find a new sense of self.

To consult secondary sources on the *coniunctio* requires a typical maneuver in Jungian psychology, a circumambulation of the topic in question. The three books listed—Stein's *Incest and Human Love,* Jacoby's *The Analytic Encounter,* and the initial issue of the annual Jungian journal *Chiron,* devoted to transference/countertransference—are all important contributions to the literature and bear closely on the extended symbolism of the *coniunctio,* its incestuous symbolism, its sexual charge, its analytical meaning. Only Edinger's seminar transcript lands full on the topic, and the conversational immediacy of the text helps greatly in making one of Jung's more challenging ideas clear and relevant.

To Begin

"On the Psychology of the Transference," cw 16, pp. 163–323.

To Go Deeper

Mysterium Coniunctionis, cw 14, esp. part 6, "The Conjunction," pp. 457–553.

Related Works

"The Transcendent Function," cw 8, pp. 67–91.
"Concerning Rebirth," cw 9, I, pp. 113–147.

Secondary Sources

Stein, Robert. *Incest and Human Love: The Betrayal of the Soul in Psychotherapy.* New York: The Third Press, 1973.

Jacoby, Mario. *The Analytic Encounter: Transference and Human Relationship*. Toronto: Inner City Books, 1984.

Schwartz-Salant, Nathan, and Stein, Murray, eds. *Chiron: A Review of Jungian Analysis*, 1984.

Edinger, Edward F. *The Mystery of the Coniunctio: Alchemical Image of Individuation*. Toronto: Inner City Books, 1994.

PART THREE

TOPICS OF
SPECIAL INTEREST

29. FREUD AND
PSYCHOANALYSIS

Much has been and will continue to be written about the relationship between Freud and Jung, for their relationship and their break with one another are one of the more significant theoretical and personal events in the history of modern psychology. However, the pyschoanalytic writings contained in Jung's *Collected Works* give simply the theoretical side of this extraordinary relationship without much of the personal relationship that informed so much of their collaboration. For an excellent and concise account of the personal history between the two men, William McGuire's introduction to *The Freud/Jung Letters* is recommended.

Jung first became acquainted with Freud by way of *The Interpretation of Dreams,* a book whose publication date of 1900 has as much symbolic as historical significance. Jung was working as a psychiatrist at the Burghölzli Hospital in Zurich, a hospital directed at that time by Eugen Bleuler, whose own work was to be profoundly influenced by Freud. Jung's writings from 1902 to 1906, such as Jung's doctoral dissertation, "On the Psychology of So-Called Occult Phenomena" (CW 1), and his numerous reports of his word association experiments (CW 2), contain a number of references to Freud's work, and Jung clearly held Freud's work in great respect. The two men began a correspondence with one another in 1906 which continued until 1914, dates that mark a period in which Freud and Jung worked closely together to make known Freud's discoveries on the causes and treatment of neurosis. Indeed, the two men traveled to the United States together for the Clark Lectures in 1912, though the growing tension between them was signaled by an episode on board ship. As Jung tells the story in his autobiography, Jung permitted Freud to analyze one of Jung's dreams while Freud refused Jung the corresponding analysis of a dream of his own, a refusal reportedly made by Freud on the grounds that it would threaten his authority. "At that moment," Jung writes, "he had lost it altogether."

Their differences over Freud's psychological theories as well as the tension between their own disparate personalities continued to grow more and more pointed over the next two years as psychoanalysis battled for professional respect in Europe. Jung's publication of *Symbols of Transformation,* which deals with the unconscious from a markedly different standpoint from Freud's, in a sense represented the culmination of their growing disaffection and indicates the very profound differences between their two psychologies. When Jung broke off his friendship with Freud in 1913 and resigned from the presidency of the International Association of Psychoanalysis in 1914, a long period of professional isolation and personal soul-searching ensued, the fruit of which was a great deal of inner wisdom and, more practically speaking, the publication of *Psychological Types* in 1921.

From that point onward, Jung's work, though indebted in certain ways to Freud, became distinctly and irrevocably at odds with the orthodox psychoanalytic theory propounded by Freud. Jung took great issue with Freud's placement of sexuality as the root cause of neurosis and thought that the single-minded emphasis on sexuality within psychoanalysis as *the* primary motive-force in psychological development was unfounded. Because of the centrality of sexuality within psychoanalytic theory, much of Jung's writings on psychoanalysis within the *Collected Works* focus on the relative importance or

unimportance of sexuality. Jung found the concept of ortho-
doxy within psychoanalytic circles oppressive and unscientific
in the extreme, and he held the opinion, stated more than
once, that dogma was more appropriate in church pronounce-
ments than in the theories of a modern science. Since Jung's
theory of personality types grew largely from his experience
with Freud and from his wish to explain divergent theories concerning the same empirically observed psychological phenomena, one is given license to observe that Jung's writings may be
evidence that Jung and Freud were quite different characters
typologically—Jung the introverted intuitive, Freud quite the
extroverted thinker.

Equally valid, however, is Jung's claim that his career was
established before his acquaintance with Freud and that he had
already developed a number of ideas of his own which were not
derived from Freud's psychoanalytic theories. The two most important examples of Jung's influence on Freudian theory are
the concept of the complex, which grew out of Jung's word
association work, and Jung's insistence that the practitioners of
psychoanalysis be analyzed themselves. Thus, however inter-
twined their careers were at a certain historical moment, Jung
began and ended his relationship with Freud, personally and
theoretically, an independent thinker in his own right.

Volume 4 of the *Collected Works,* entitled *Freud and Psychoanalysis,* brings together Jung's major writings from the periods
during and after his association with Freud. The major piece in
the volume, "The Theory of Psychoanalysis," was written as a
series of nine lectures and is indicated under "To Begin" because it provides an excellent basic overview of Jung's psychoanalytic views in an extended, well-organized fashion. The rest
of this volume consists of bits and pieces of Jung's writings on
psychoanalysis, which have been organized here under "To Go
Deeper" to show the stages of Jung's thought concerning
Freudian theory: papers that show him to be in general agree-

ment and indeed at times even an apologist for Freud and psychoanalytic theory; followed by papers in which Jung hazards a
fair bit of criticism of Freudian concepts; and finally papers
that show Jung to have broken fully with Freud, some of which
are surprisingly strongly worded. Those papers that focus on
technical responses to various critics or writers have been omit-
ted here; the more scholarly reader will probably find these of
more interest than will the general public. The correspondence between Jung and Löy should be noted and read because of the way it reveals a more relaxed and down-to-earth
Jung than the one we generally see in his formal publications.
Also included are two short pieces Jung wrote concerning
Freud, which, while not particularly penetrating or enlighten-
ing, have a certain amount of historical interest.

Jung's autobiography is listed here because of the account
it includes of his relationship to Freud, while Liliane Frey-
Rohn's volume tackles the material theoretically, providing a
point-by-point comparison of the major ideas in Jungian and
Freudian psychology. The volume of letters between Freud and
Jung—a volume whose creation resembled nothing so much
as a disarmament conference between two superpowers—must
also be read for the best possible knowledge of these two great
men, their relationship, and their failure to remain friends and
colleagues.

To Begin

 The Theory of Psychoanalysis, CW 4, pp. 83–226.

To Go Deeper

 "The Freudian Theory of Hysteria," CW 4, pp. 10–24.
 "The Analysis of Dreams," CW 4, pp. 25–34.
 "A Contribution to the Psychology of Rumour," CW 4, pp. 35–47.
 "On the Criticism of Psychoanalysis," CW 4, pp. 74–77.

"Concerning Psychoanalysis," CW 4, pp. 78–81.

"General Aspects of Psychoanalysis," CW 4, pp. 229–242.

"Psychoanalysis and Neurosis," CW 4, pp. 243–251.

"Some Crucial Points in Psychoanalysis: A Correspondence between Dr. Jung and Dr. Löy," CW 4, pp. 252–289.

"Introduction to Kranefeldt's *Secret Ways of the Mind*," CW 4, pp. 324–332.

"Freud and Jung: Contrasts," CW 4, pp. 333–340.

"Freud in his Historical Setting," CW 15, pp. 33–40.

"In Memory of Sigmund Freud," CW 15, pp. 41–49.

"Depth Psychology," CW 18, pp. 477–486.

Related Works

"On Psychological Understanding," CW 3, pp. 179–193.

"The Psychology of Dementia Praecox," CW 3, pp. 1–151.

Secondary Sources

Jung, C. G., with Jaffé Aniela. *Memories, Dreams, Reflections*. New York: Vintage Books, 1965.

McGuire, William, ed. *The Freud/Jung Letters: The Correspondence between Sigmund Freud and C. G. Jung*. Princeton: Princeton University Press, 1974.

Frey-Rohn, Liliane. *From Freud to Jung: A Comparative Study of the Psychology of the Unconscious*. New York: C.G. Jung Foundation for Analytical Psychology, 1974.

30. SCHIZOPHRENIA

Jung's writings on schizophrenia represent a major portion of his earliest work and form an important part of the early twentieth-century psychiatric literature on this mental disease. In his work at Burghölzli Hospital in Zurich under Eugen Bleuler and as Bleuler's successor to the directorship there, Jung was intimately involved with the treatment of what was then called dementia praecox or precocious senility. Since the symptoms of this diesease—hallucinations, delusions, odd mannerisms, social withdrawal, and disordered thought—formed the very definition of insanity at that time, Bleuler's work was instrumental in bringing some order to the clinical formulations concerning this condition, which Bleuler renamed schizophrenia. Bleuler had come to understand schizophrenia, not as a single uniform mental disease, but rather as a group of varied but usually chronically psychotic syndromes, and further, he saw that these syndromes were all characterized by a fragmentation of consciousness—thus, the "split brain" of his nomenclature, so often interpreted to mean multiple or split personality.

While working under Bleuler, Jung was introduced to Freud and Breuer's work on hysteria; in particular, the publication of Freud's masterwork, *The Interpretation of Dreams,* gave Jung yet another piece of the psychological puzzle concerning schizophrenia, a piece that had been indicated by Jung's own word association experiments: the realization that schizophrenia could not be simply an organic disease of the mind, but that a nonorganic, psychological component lay behind much of the seemingly senseless psychotic symptomatology. Using

Freud's insights into the nature of unconscious process and conflicts, along with his own concept of the autonomous feeling-toned complex, Jung spent much time and effort attempting to trace down the psychological and emotional causes for schizophrenia through meticulous history-taking from his patients and by scrupulous attention to the details of their illness. Thus, Jung did for psychotic patients what Freud and Breuer had done for hysterics, showing that the insane behavior of the schizophrenic was actually the expression of intolerable emotional conflicts, an upwelling of unconscious complexes that then swamp the individual ego and render the patient cognitively and behaviorally out of touch with reality.

For this reason, Jung understood that the bizarre symptoms of psychotic patients, though obviously more severe and debilitating for schizophrenics, were in fact not that dissimilar from what one saw in normal or neurotic patients: symbolic expressions of unconscious material. In the context of the medical thought of that period, this psychoanalytic interpretation of schizophrenia was quite revolutionary, even though Jung at all times agreed with the accepted notion, held then and supported today by voluminous research and experience, that some kind of organic chemical factor must also be involved in the onset of schizophrenia. Jung's contribution to understanding schizophrenia, therefore, is among the more significant works of modern psychology, synthesizing psychoanalytic and medical thought with his own ideas drawn from his early psychiatric career.

Volume 3 of the *Collected Works* brings together all of Jung's writings on the topic, including a number of short lectures and papers on schizophrenia that were written after his break with Freud. All of these papers, including his major work on the topic, "On the Problem of Psychogenesis in Mental Disease," are surprisingly relevant and readable given the dates they were written. Two exceptions must be noted here, however: The first part of the paper just mentioned contains an intricate and no longer very useful review of the literature on schizophrenia from the turn of the century, and the paper entitled "On Psychological Understanding," though published in connection with one of Jung's papers on schizophrenia, is a philosophical-epistemological excursus that actually has little to do with schizophrenia. With these two exceptions in mind and armed with a certain familiarity with Jung's concept of the complex, one may read the papers contained in this volume quite profitably as organized. The rough chronological order of these pieces gives one a sense of the development of Jung's thought on schizophrenia through and beyond his association with psychoanalysis.

John Weir Perry is perhaps the best-known Jungian analyst to have followed Jung's lead concerning the meaning and treatment of psychosis. His two books stand as the major contributions to the subject in the Jungian literature. The collection of recent papers on psychosis and its treatment is included, as well, proving the perennial usefulness of Jung's attitudes and techniques.

To Begin

"The Psychology of Dementia Praecox," CW 3, pp. 1–151.
"The Content of the Psychoses," CW 3, pp. 153–178.

To Go Deeper

"A Criticism of Bleuler's Theory of Schizophrenic Negativism," CW 3, pp. 197–202.
"On the Importance of the Unconscious in Psychopathology," CW 3, pp. 203–210.
"On the Problem of Psychogenesis in Mental Disease," CW 3, pp. 211–225.
"Mental Disease and the Psyche," CW 3, pp. 226–230.

"On the Psychogenesis of Schizophrenia," cw 3, pp. 233–249.

"Recent Thoughts on Schizophrenia," cw 3, pp. 250–255.

"Schizophrenia," cw 3, pp. 256–272.

Related Works

Elsewhere in this book, see the readings lists in chapter 2, "Complex," and chapter 16, "Ego."

Secondary Sources

Perry, John Weir, *The Self in Psychotic Process*. Dallas: Spring Publications, 1953, 1987.

Perry, John Weir. *The Far Side of Madness*. Englewood Cliffs, N.J.: Prentice-Hall, 1974.

Killick, Katherine, and Schaverien, Jay, eds. *Art, Psychotherapy and Psychosis*. London: Routledge, 1997.

31. CHILD DEVELOPMENT
AND PSYCHOLOGY

Unlike psychoanalytic theory, with its focus on etiology and the influence of infantile trauma on subsequent psychosexual development, Jung's theoretical positions took him out of the realm of childhood as the sole basis for psychological study, since Jung considered psychological development a lifelong phenomenon, not a task completed by the end of puberty. Jung consequently wrote little on child development and psychology compared to the massive and continuing interest in childhood and child analysis in Freudian circles. The articles on child development and psychology within the *Collected Works* were written largely in response to invitations extended to Jung as a major psychologist of his time to speak to various conventions of educators on his own psychological theories and their application to education. This situation thus lends these writings a certain accessibility that many other of Jung's writings do not have, as these were written mainly for lay audiences interested in the application of psychological understanding.

Among Jung's major ideas on child psychology and development is that the normal child lives psychologically in a state of unconsciousness from which various isolated moments of consciousness appear, like islands in a sea, and that such islands of consciousness gradually grow larger and larger until the ego complex eventually crystallizes and allows for more or less continuous conscious awareness of self and others. Though Jung could not help but acknowledge the various psychological disturbances that afflict children at points in their development, he saw many, if not most, of these disturbances as due more to the child's absorption of conflicts from the parents' repressed or denied unconscious material rather than to any disturbance inherent in the child. Jung therefore found it more helpful to have the parents of a disturbed child in analysis rather than to treat the child alone, and his case reports of work with children reflect his opinion that the causes of a child's disturbance are to be found in the unconscious of the adults around the child.

In the childhood state of unconsciousness, which Jung considered normal, Jung saw an image of the collective or racial unconscious. His theory that the individual human being recapitulates in his or her individual psychological development the stages that the species has gone through in its psychological development as a whole is thus applied to children whose unconscious state permits them access to the collective unconscious of all humanity in a way that adults subsequently lose through the development of ego. Just as unconsciousness precedes consciousness collectively, so, too, it is in the stages of individual development. Hence, Jung considered many of the symbols in children's dreams and games to be the direct expression of material from the collective unconscious and, as such, extremely valuable in enhancing our knowledge of this stratum of shared psychic experience.

The reading list is organized based on the idea that Jung's reports of what he *did* with children in analysis are more readable, at least initially, than his *theories* about child development and analysis. Under "To Begin," therefore, one finds three case studies of Jung's work with children; "To Go Deeper" then includes the more conceptual, theoretical material in the *Collected Works*.

Certain of Jung's followers have taken his theories on childhood development and psychology much further than the articles in the *Collected Works* did, developing therapeutic tech-

niques for both adults and children, most notably sandtray
therapy, which seek to bring to consciousness the symbols of
the collective unconscious so prominent in the psychology of
children: Dora Kalff is most noted in this regard. While somewhat dated, Frances G. Wickes's book *The Inner World of Childhood* gives a good view of more classic Jungian thought on the
psychology and the development of the child; Jung's foreword
to the German edition of her book is included in volume 17 of
the *Collected Works* and noted in the following list.

To Begin

"Psychic Conflicts in a Child," CW 17, pp. 1–35.
"A Contribution to the Psychology of Rumour," CW 4, pp. 35–47.
The Theory of Psychoanalysis, CW 4, esp. part 9, "A Case of Neurosis
in a Child," pp. 204–226.

To Go Deeper

"Analytical Psychology and Education," CW 17, pp. 65–132.
"Child Development and Education," CW 17, pp. 49–62.
"The Gifted Child," CW 17, pp. 133–145.
"The Significance of the Unconscious in Individual Education,"
CW 17, pp. 149–164.
"The Development of Personality," CW 17, pp. 165–186.

Related Works

"The Significance of the Father in the Destiny of the Individual,"
CW 4, pp. 301–323.
"Psychological Aspects of the Mother Archetype," CW 9, I,
pp. 75–110.

Secondary Sources

Kalff, Dora M. *Sandplay: A Psychotherapeutic Approach to the Psyche.*
Boston: Sigo Press, 1980.
Wickes, Frances G. *The Inner World of Childhood.* 3d ed. Boston: Sigo
Press, 1988.

32. LOVE AND MARRIAGE

However broad Jung's psychological purview, however transformative his psychological vision, however important his introversion, he nevertheless was a man who lived a comparatively normal everyday life as well. Married to a strong and intelligent woman who often functioned as professional colleague and emotional support, father of six children, intimate friend to many men and women, teacher and guide to many of his analysands, Jung was hardly the reclusive Wise Old Man secreted away in his study poring over ancient manuscripts and churning out mystical texts. On the contrary, Jung was a man at the center of many important, lifelong relationships and so, at various times, he put pen to paper to describe that which occurs *between* people and not simply that which occurs within the individual soul.

His writings on love and marriage, while atypical of his larger body of work, nevertheless make use of his concept of the anima/animus projection to explain how an initial surge of mutual attraction may be related more to a projected part of oneself being seen in another rather than to true relatedness. Though Jung understood projection as the concept is generally understood—namely, the unconscious ascription of qualities, feelings, or thoughts of one's own to another—he also saw projection as more valuable than a simple defense mechanism against unacceptable impulses or thoughts. Through projection, the psyche is able to continually present to the individual that which exists within oneself but which has yet to be made conscious or integrated. In this manner, projection serves the

143

tendency toward wholeness of the psyche by providing oppor-
tunities to integrate the opposites that are being split and projected onto other things and people.

Essential to the course of analysis and obviously to the
process of individuation is distinguishing between one's projections onto others and one's own inner qualities and dynamics,
with the goal of withdrawing the power of the projected qualities from others and integrating these aspects into one's own
sense of self. Such a task, Jung makes clear, is essential for true
relatedness to another as well, since true relatedness is possible
only after the often laborious (and sometimes painful) process
of peeling away mutual projections has been accomplished, re-
vealing the other person in all his or her reality. Ever prag-
matic, Jung acknowledges that many relationships would not
survive such a process and often do not, ending either in a
breakup or in a kind of psychological accommodation in which
true intimacy is forfeited for comfort or security.

Thus, Jung introduces the concept of the container and
the contained within a marriage relationship to describe this
dynamic of psychological accommodation—how one partner's
strength permits the other partner's weakness, how one provides the strong container while the other falls into the role of
the dependent, contained participant in the relationship—
with the result, of course, that the infantile parent-child relationship is re-created and both members of the couple suffer
from a kind of institutionalized psychological immaturity. In
Jung's writings on love and marriage, what comes through
most clearly is the need for both participants in a couple to be
psychologically individuated for true intimacy to occur and the
danger to true relationship posed by the unconscious adoption
of collective forms of relationship, such as marriage. As the
center of individuation is both consciousness and choice, both
of these qualities may be put at the greatest risk or may be the

instruments of the greatest possible transformation of life when it comes to love and marriage.

While these issues obviously are raised in Jung's many discussions of the anima/animus and of Eros and Logos, the two papers by Jung which focus on these issues most clearly from an outward perspective are "Marriage as a Psychological Relationship" and "The Love Problem of a Student." "Woman in Europe" is indicated for further exploration because of the way these issues are touched by Jung in his discussions of the social and psychological position of women in modern society. Secondary sources include Adolf Guggenbühl-Craig's well-known examination of these issues; Polly Young-Eisendrath's more provocative, Jungian-feminist approach to couple therapy; Linda Leonard's popular exploration of the love relationship from a Jungian-symbolic perspective; and, finally, a work by John Desteian, Jungian analyst and divorce mediator.

To Begin

"Marriage as a Psychological Relationship," cw 17, pp. 189–201.
"The Love Problem of a Student," cw 10, pp. 97–112.

To Go Deeper

"Woman in Europe," cw 10, pp. 113–133.

Related Works

Elsewhere in this book, see the readings lists in chapter 9, "Eros and Logos/Masculine and Feminine," and chapter 19, "Anima/Animus."

Secondary Sources

Guggenbühl-Craig, Adolf. *Marriage—Dead or Alive.* Dallas: Spring Publications, 1977.

Young-Eisendrath, Polly. *Hags and Heroes: A Feminist Approach to Couple Psychotherapy*. Toronto: Inner City Books, 1984.

Leonard, Linda. *On the Way to the Wedding*. Boston: Shambhala, 1986.

Desteian, John. *Coming Apart/Coming Together: The Union of Opposites in Love Relationships*. Boston: Sigo Press, 1988.

33. OCCULT PHENOMENA

Along with his interest in flying saucers, alchemy, and synchronistic occurrences, Jung's interest in occult phenomena has often been misunderstood and erroneously characterized as naive, unscientific, and trivial. Undeniable is Jung's attention to what he termed, quite significantly, "so-called occult phenomena," such as ghosts, apparitions, uncanny visions, mediumistic or spiritualistic demonstrations such as trances, table-rapping, levitation, automatic writing, and what would nowadays be called the channeling of disembodied spirits or deceased persons. Jung's doctoral dissertation, "On the Psychology and Pathology of So-Called Occult Phenomena," contained in volume 1 of the *Collected Works,* was in fact a study of his cousin's mediumistic abilities and was one of the first demonstrations of Jung's enduring interest in the weird and irrational.

What many people often do not appreciate, though, is Jung's attitude toward such occult phenomena. Far from being credulous, Jung developed psychological theories concerning the causation of such phenomena which, if anything, lead to a thorough debunking of the literal claims of such mediums. While ostensibly channeling and contacting the spirits from beyond, these psychics, in Jung's opinion, are simply channeling unconscious contents of their own split-off and autonomous complexes of extraordinary power and vividness. These complexes, Jung posits, are the occult spirits responsible for many of the attention-grabbing occurrences and the uncanny visions reported by so many people. The title of Jung's dissertation makes clear that these phenomena may be *called* occult but often are demonstrations of psychological states that may be pathological or hysterical. Since Jung begins his dissertation by listing examples of such spiritualistic behavior in cases that range from the slightly disturbed to the frankly psychopathic, his skeptical psychiatric interest in these phenomena is made amply clear.

While Jung certainly leaves open the door to subsequent proof of the reality of these rappings and tappings, he nevertheless takes a firmly rational, psychological stance toward these events, a position that may well dismay many present-day New Age spiritualists who perceive in Jung's writings support for many transpersonal claims but who might not feel so at home with Jung after reading his actual writings on the subject. Despite his doubting posture toward these occurrences, Jung never for a moment dismisses the *psychological* reality of these phenomena, seeing within these beliefs, sightings, and events images that point toward symbols of collective unconscious, symbols whose irrational but undeniable effects cannot— indeed, must not—be underestimated. Moreover, with his theory of synchronocity, put forth later in his career, Jung provides further subjective, psychological explanations for unusual, seemingly occult coincidences or occurrences, viewing these events as essentially acausal, a view that further undermines the cause-and-effect magical thinking of so many occult practitioners.

To investigate in a rational manner phenomena that are fundamentally irrational may be a difficult scientific feat to pull off successfully. The reader may judge the success of Jung's writings on the occult. Under "To Begin" I list Jung's dissertation and a short comment on it, while under "To Go Deeper" I recommend a collection of short pieces and forewords to various books in which Jung continues his discussions on spiritualistic phenomena.

Since the concern with life after death is a consistent characteristic of much occult thought and practice, I also note two books on the subject of life after death by Aniela Jaffé and Marie-Louise von Franz, longtime associates of Jung, who treat the subject from a typically Jungian (that is to say, psychological) viewpoint. Sallie Nichols's book *Jung and Tarot* demonstrates how Jung's insights into the nature and function of unconscious symbolism may be applied psychologically, rather than in a naive fortunetelling way, to the use of tarot cards.

To Begin

"On the Psychology and the Pathology of So-Called Occult Phenomena," CW 1, pp. 3–88.

"On Hysterical Misreading," CW 1, pp. 89–92.

To Go Deeper

"On Occultism," CW 18, pp. 291–329.

Related Works

"The Spiritual Problem of Modern Man," CW 10, pp. 74–94.

"The Soul and Death," CW 8, pp. 404–415.

"Synchronicity: An Acausal Connecting Principle," CW 8, pp. 417–531.

Secondary Sources

Jaffé, Aniela. *Apparitions: An Archetypal Approach to Death Dreams and Ghosts.* Dallas: Spring Publications, 1979.

Von Franz, Marie-Louise. *On Dreams and Death.* Boston: Shambhala, 1986. Chicago: Open Court, 1997.

Nichols, Sallie. *Jung and Tarot: An Archetypal Journey.* York Beach, Maine: Samuel Weiser, 1980.

34. UFO

The metaphor of the guided tour of the *Collected Works* was chosen deliberately, since in reading the collection of Jung's writings one can feel as if one is wandering about in a great European city where, upon turning a particular corner, something quite unusual and fascinating appears, something typical for the time and place and yet something extraordinary and very different. Jung's writings on unidentified flying objects, or UFOs, may represent just such an intriguing find on our tour of his writings. Jung's interest in the uncanny and the unexplainable, or as he might put it, the irrational, was a lifelong characteristic, beginning with his earliest writings on occult phenomena, stretching through the major period of his writing and his researches into mythology and alchemy, and moving at the end of his life toward modern examples of the mythic imagination at work. Unfortunately, Jung's interest in such irrational psychic phenomena is often misunderstood as credulous or unsophisticated, but Jung's writings on flying saucers exemplify once more certain characteristics of his approach to such phenomena.

Jung's focus, first, foremost, and always, is psychological. His purpose in examining the various reports of flying saucers—"things seen in the skies"—is not to establish the truth or falsehood of these reports but rather to inquire into the psychological meaning of such reports for the individuals involved or for the larger culture. This psychological focus does not require that Jung believe that visitors from another planet are actually visiting Earth, nor does it require that he refute these claims. For Jung's psychological focus, that individuals believe that they saw what they saw in the skies is sufficient. Thus, whether or not flying saucers actually exist, Jung holds that such things, even if literally untrue, are nevertheless psychic facts amenable to psychological, symbolic investigation.

Second and equally characteristic, Jung examines the possibility that such worldwide UFO sightings hold a collective meaning, a mythic importance for modern people. For this reason, Jung unearths in the most surprising way parallel images and sightings from mythology and historical reports. He draws this material not as credulous ufologist seeking to establish the objective reality of flying saucers. He instead uses these historical and collective amplifications to wonder aloud about the significance of such sightings at the current moment in history. What is it from the unconscious that, because denied, repressed, or not fully appreciated, seems to be projected on the physical world and is seen as strange, alien and frightening? What is seeking to contact us from within? Jung therefore treats reports of UFOs as one might treat dreams: worthy of investigation, pregnant with psychological meaning, connected to the collective history of the human condition.

The articles dealing with these sightings make clear that Jung sees UFOs as symbols of the Self, especially because of the mandalalike shape of so many of these alien spaceships. Given the historical period of these sightings—immediately following the worldwide fragmentation and psychic dislocation caused by World War II—the appearance of the Self in these mysterious sightings is Jung's unique hypothesis and his addition to the growing literature on these close encounters. In light of this hypothesis, one might wonder what the current popular reports mean, since they have gone far beyond mere sightings in the skies and are now rife with stories of actual contacts with extraterrestrials, abductions by aliens, forced experimentation in spaceships from another world, and entire spiritual communities founded and structured around the belief in UFOs. If the popular mythology of UFOs is centered on manifestations of the Self, one may wonder if the current state of UFO reports is a progression to a greater sense of relationship to the universe as a whole or a regressive, determined projection of that wholeness outside of ourselves onto the boundless skies above.

Interestingly enough, no works by Jungian analysts follow Jung's lead in investigating the symbolic meaning of UFO sightings. Certainly the demands of creating a workable therapeutic psychology and the enormous task of research into the mythology of the past has left little time for analysts to devote to the mythology of current popular culture. Perhaps the third generation of Jungian analysts will make a substantial contribution to illuminating what exactly we think we see coming from beyond us in these altogether uncanny sightings in the heavens.

To Begin

"Flying Saucers: A Modern Myth of Things Seen in the Skies," cw 10, pp. 307–433.

To Go Deeper

"On Flying Saucers," cw 18, pp. 626–633.

Related Works

Psychological Types, cw 6, esp. chap. 11, "Definitions," under "Self," pp. 460–461.

"Concerning Mandala Symbolism," cw 9, I, pp. 355–384.

35. MODERN ART AND ART CRITICISM

Volume 15 of the *Collected Works* contains a quartet of short pieces that Jung wrote concerning art, a quartet that actually is made of two duets, so to speak: a pair of articles on the general question of the relationship between art and psychology and another pair of articles in which Jung applied his psychological understanding to two great artists of the twentieth century, James Joyce and Pablo Picasso. The lack of any extended work on this topic by Jung and the fact that three of these four pieces were written on request is evidence that the relationship between art and psychology was hardly of consuming interest for Jung. Yet one has the sense that, given the extensive critical use to which Freudian psychoanalytic theory had been put, Jung felt obliged to put forth his own view, especially since in the course of his career he had seen how central and transformative symbol-making was for the human soul.

On the relationship between art and psychology, Jung pleads once again that one abandon an analytic-reductive approach to creative work and encounter a work of art on its own terms instead of searching for the psychological causes of any work of art. Furthermore, Jung separates the psychology of the individual artist from the validity of that artist's creative work, which, in Jung's mind, stands or falls on the merits of its own achievements, rather than being judged by the sanity or neuroticism of the artist and creator. Both these positions are in some ways not so veiled responses to forays into art criticism

made by Freud and his followers, and Jung seems quite at
home with the realization that great artists are almost always
exceptional individuals for whom normal psychological categories may not apply. Given Jung's own copious creative output
over the course of his lifetime, the issue of artistic creativity, its
psychological cost, and its value for the individual and collective life, was clearly one Jung had lived from the inside for
many, many years.

The paper on Joyce's *Ulysses* has a fascinating history described in the appendix to the version in the *Collected Works;* the
appendix actually may be of more interest than the paper itself,
which is largely a chronicle of Jung's difficulties in making
sense of Joyce's stream of consciousness style. Jung's paper on
Picasso is equally interesting but hardly revolutionary. One has
the sense that, however innovative and forward-looking Jung's
psychology, Jung the man had a difficult time gaining entry
into the world of these two archetypally modern artists, as if
Jung still lived in the world of the nineteenth century while
Joyce and Picasso were programmatically dismantling this
world to depict the true character of the twentieth century,
with its lack of meaning, its disorder, its anomie, it breakdown
of communication and knowledge. The ease with which Jung
can grasp the psychological meaning of such other, older liter-
ary works as Goethe's *Faust,* Spitteler's *Prometheus and Epimeth-
eus,* or Nietzsche's *Also sprach Zarathustra* lends support to this
observation. While Jung acknowledges this modern breakdown
of meaning—indeed, this breakdown is a major concern for
him throughout his writings as a psychologist—Jung's contribution to the cure and understanding of the twentieth century
malaise is not in art criticism but in psychology. All the same,
Jung's insights in these four articles and in his other writings
on the nature and the function of the symbol form the basis
for subsequent attempts by Jung's followers to draw out the
psychological implications of various works of art, from paint-

ing to film, in the spirit of Jung's psychology, concerned with the positive, transformative effect of symbol-making on the life of the soul. Erich Neumann's two collections of essays on art and creativity stand as classics in Jungian thought and should be read. Contemporary views are represented by two books, one a collection of conference papers, the other a very thought-provoking and unusual use of Jung's thought. For more samples of contemporary ways Jung's notions are applied to art and culture, any of the four Jungian journals in the United States are highly recommended. These periodicals almost always include some analytical psychological treatment of a creative work, be it a book, a movie, an opera, or an art exhibit. The interested reader is urged to consult these journals to see how Jungian psychological insight is being applied to contemporary art and culture.

To Begin

"On the Relation of Analytical Psychology to Poetry," cw 15, pp. 65–83.

"Psychology and Literature," cw 15, pp. 84–105.

To Go Deeper

" 'Ulysses': A Monologue," cw 15, pp. 109–134.

"Picasso," cw 15, pp. 135–141.

Related Works

Elsewhere in this book, see the readings lists in Chapter 6, "Active Imagination," and chapter 13, "Individuation."

Secondary Sources

Neumann, Erich. *Art and the Creative Unconscious.* London: Routledge & Kegan Paul, 1959.

Neumann, Erich. *Creative Man.* Princeton: Princeton University Press, 1979.

Barnaby, Karen, and D'Acierno, Pellegrino. *C. G. Jung and the Humanities: Toward a Hermeneutics of Culture.* Princeton: Princeton University Press, 1990.

Philipson, Morris. *An Outline of Jungian Aesthetics.* Boston: Sigo, 1963, 1994.

Psychological Perspectives: A Semi-Annual Review of Jungian Thought, published by the C. G. Jung Institute of Los Angeles.

Quadrant, published semi-annually by the C. G. Jung Foundation, New York.

The San Francisco Jung Institute Library Journal, published quarterly.

Spring, published annually by Spring Publications, Woodstock, Conn.

PART FOUR

ESOTERICA

INTRODUCTION

This part is devoted to those volumes of the *Collected Works* which the lay reader may not at first be particularly interested in or prepared to read. In terming these works esoteric, the intention is not to frighten off the nonspecialist but rather to point to the extraordinary character of these works and their subject matter. These works demand a thorough-going knowledge of Jung's writings as a whole and a taste for scholarly writing on subjects many would characterize as mystical or philosophical. As such, the four volumes presented in this section are not essentially volumes to sit down and read in the manner of many of Jung's other writings; rather, they are works to be consulted and studied, to be taken in and savored little by little, rather than devoured and digested all in a piece (as if that were possible!), writings to return to and read a number of times, rather than master and assimilate quickly and easily. The prose is what I have come to call image-dense, full of symbolic interconnections and historical-psychological allusions, packed with imagistic minutiae; one can safely say that the reader completely unfamiliar with Jung will probably not get very far in these works, even with the extensive introduction and suggestions that follow. However, because Jung consistently weds his diverse explorations to his principal goal—namely, knowledge of the psyche in all its wonder and wealth—these esoteric works are ultimately accessible to the assiduous and interested reader, who will find in them a cache of psychological and spiritual riches. Since the majority of these works represent Jung's thought toward the end of his life and career, they

constitute an invaluable summing-up of analytical psychology
with which any serious student of Jung should be familiar.

Three of these volumes concern alchemy, a topic of lifelong interest to Jung, whose knowledge of alchemical writings
may be safely described as unique in modern psychology. The
extensive nature of Jung's interest in alchemy requires an
equally extensive introduction, and the complicated, erudite
character of his alchemical writings makes it necessary to introduce each of the three "alchemical" volumes of the *Collected
Works* separately. The fourth volume to be introduced here is
Aion, an equally erudite and detailed examination of Christian
symbolism in a psychological context.

36. JUNG AND ALCHEMY

As any reader can see in looking at the *Collected Works* on a shelf, volume 12, *Psychology and Alchemy*, volume 13, *Alchemical Studies*, and volume 14, *Mysterium Coniunctionis*, constitute a sizable portion of Jung's writings, and the physical space these volumes occupy accurately indicates the significance of alchemical symbolism in Jung's thought. Jung's formulations on the nature of the psyche, his continued attention to psychic processes, and his own experiences of archetypal transformation led him to see in alchemical imagery and symbolism a language, a mode of thought, and a method whose history, development, and spiritual-psychological focus closely mirrored his own understandings. Alchemical imagery had certain advantages, however, that in Jung's opinion much modern psychological terminology did not have.

First, contrary to certain mistaken ideas about Jung, his interest in alchemy was never based on his belief in the literal truth of certain alchemist's claims, for example, that they could turn lead into gold or carry out other improbable chemical-physical transformations. Jung's attention, instead, was devoted primarily to what he called philosophical alchemy, that is, the writings of those alchemists whose descriptions of chemical procedures were specifically intended and acknowledged to be statements of spiritual and philosophical truths. Far from accepting alchemical claims, Jung discerned that, within the complicated physicochemical descriptions of these medieval texts, the alchemists were projecting psychic qualities and processes of their own onto the physical substances and procedures and

161

then described these phenomena *as if* they were occurring out-side of themselves in the substances they were manipulating.

Though Jung acknowledged that many of the alchemical texts were in fact nothing more than chemical recipes or exam-ples of obscure thinking, he nevertheless saw quite clearly that many alchemists did not limit their field of vision to the mere transformation of base physical matter and were attempting to provide, on the basis of their own inner experiences, a kind of psychological, philosophical, and spiritual system, a discipline of soul, mind, and matter, which would lead to the complete transformation of the individual alchemist himself. Moreover, Jung's unique and comprehensive acquaintance with these texts enabled him to point out which alchemists were quite explicit in their philosophical intentions, realizing themselves that their gold was not "common gold" but a spiritual gold, stating that their art was as much "ethical as physical."

For Jung's purposes, therefore, alchemy was a perfect mar-riage, a highly elaborate philosophical and psychological sys-tem whose language was first and foremost symbolic and imaginal, in contrast to the dry, technical scientific language with which psychology had been saddled since the Enlighten-ment. Jung found within alchemical imagery a source and me-dium for expressing many of his own psychological insights, which he had gleaned through his own introspection and his analytic work with patients, and his writings provide testimony to the centrality of alchemical imagery in his thinking. Many standard terms within Jungian psychology are drawn straight from alchemical writings: the characterization of analytical work as an *opus;* the reference to the analytic relationship as a *vas,* vessel or container; the goal of the analytic process as the *coniunctio,* or union of conflicting opposites; and the opposi-tion of solar and lunar consciousness, to name just a few.

Second, alchemy possessed a long and complex history and represented a continuing stream of unorthodox, underground culture within Western civilization. Alchemy and its symbolic language, therefore, carried all the cultural weight of the Western unconscious mind—which was precisely Jung's lifework—and it did so in a form relatively uncontaminated with what Jung considered the psychological distortions of Christian dogma. Thus, alchemical writings, for all their complexity, enabled Jung to tap into a pure spring of the collective unconscious, at a time and place in Western historical consciousness outside of orthodox Christian thought.

Third, Jung found that individual alchemists attempted to develop a method of working with the material and effecting transformation. Though alchemists' methods were irrational, to be sure, based as they were on psychic projections rather than on objective knowledge, Jung found a practical description of inner growth in alchemical attempts to systematize physical substances and the various stages of physical changes purported to occur in the course of the alchemical operations. These various terms also have found their way into many a description of the individuation process: *nigredo*, for the dark night of the soul, when an individual confronts the shadow within; *separatio*, for the moment of emotional and spiritual discrimination; *mortificatio* or *putrefactio*, for the stage at which the old neurotic ways of being are cast off; *dissolutio*, for the initial disorientation after the old self is discarded. As a psychotherapist, Jung found the practical nature of alchemical method a rich source of imagery for describing the highly symbolic transformations that occur in analysis.

In the writings of the medieval alchemists, Jung found an intention, a language and a method that paralleled his own modern psychological program. Alchemy and the alchemical texts Jung collected indelibly marked his thinking and his personality and those of nearly all his followers. While Jung's alchemical writings are vitally significant, the uninitiated reader of them will quickly discover that alchemy was never anything

like a unitary, cohesive field of study. Quite the contrary, alchemy was a highly individualistic enterprise with idiosyncratic
terms and images that varied from alchemist to alchemist, each
term with its own myriad meanings on multiple levels ranging
from literal to figurative to spiritual to philosophical to mystical. If the strange Latin or Greek terminology, often drawn
from Gnostic or other obscure sources, does not bog the
reader down, surely the overwhelming profusion of bizarre and
unusual imagery will present at least as formidable a challenge.
For this reason, the earnest lay reader is in an especially awkward position with regard to Jung's alchemical works: they represent some of Jung's most significant work and simultaneously
are perhaps the most difficult of his writings to truly enter into.

Certain suggestions for reading these alchemical volumes
may be useful. First, the highly impressionistic nature of the
alchemical enterprise means that logical, linear continuity is
not especially important in reading Jung's explications of alchemical imagery. One does not necessarily need to start on
page 1 and read straight through to page 500 to profit from or
understand the images or concepts. Indeed, the reading
scheme I present for each of the volumes ignores Jung's organization of the material in favor of starting first with what the
average reader will probably find most comprehensible and
grounded. However, one may want to abandon this reading
scheme altogether and simply leaf through the three volumes,
allowing one's attention to rest with whatever catches one's
eyes, reading whatever seems interesting, and studying which-
ever pictures pique one's curiosity. Reading Jung on alchemy
is not an Apollonian task, a task guided by sunlight, logic, and
linearity climbing ever upward, but rather a hermetic task, a
task of shapelessness and movement leading downward into
the semiobscurity of the ocean of the Western collective unconscious—a swim to the depths rather than a hike to the summit.
Let the individual reader be guided accordingly.

Second, if for some reason one truly wants to master this difficult area of the *Collected Works* and do it in the order in which Jung himself organized the material, then the best suggestion is to go about it slowly, allowing each image and symbol plenty of time to sink in and flourish in one's imagination, before going on to another image or discussion. Since the language of alchemy is the language of the unconscious—that mysterious and condensed symbolic language common to dreams, poetry, and artistic creation—Jung's alchemical writings should be treated similarly. Just as one does not truly profit from rushing through a museum but rather does well to go slowly and allow each work to create its own mood and impression, so, too, with each piece of the alchemical process and the psychological parallels Jung draws.

Third and finally, the true value of Jung's alchemical writings lies not in their esoteric or sheer imaginal value, but rather in their ability to provide a symbolic language for psychological and spiritual experience. Rather than attempt to carry out a typical academic process of cognitive comprehension of these works, therefore, one may do better to try to relate each alchemical image to one's own experiences, inward or outward. Though of course many of these images are hopelessly strange or fabulous, I imagine it would be rare for an individual not to find some common psychological ground, whether in dreams or in imagination. Within such a commonality, one might find also that alchemical insights challenge or amplify one's inner experience or understanding. Since, in many ways, alchemy was similar to a civilization-wide active imagination, Jung's writings might be made a bit less alien and a bit more meaningful if treated similarly, as sourcebooks for imaginative fantasy and psychological enrichment.

As is probably clear by now, these writings ask of the reader a certain commitment, an openness to understanding one's experience symbolically, and a willingness to risk becoming lost at times in the wealth of the collective unconscious. Yet the benefits of a relationship to these writings from Jung's later life repay the cost of the time and energy spent.

What follows is what one might call a program of reading in Jung and alchemy. My hope in providing the following introductions to the individual volumes is to place upon these multifaceted writings a modicum of organization, enough to indicate to the reader Jung's intentions and purposes, and to point out which volumes and sections are the best-organized and clearest within the *massa confusa* of Jung's writings (to borrow yet another alchemical term). This introduction is written for thinking types primarily, who may need to know the overall purpose and structure of the book before tackling its substance, though sensate, intuitive, and feeling types may find themselves lost at times and may wish to use the following program as a kind of orienting map. As already mentioned, Jung often did not organize his material in a way I have found helpful to the lay reader, and so I have chosen to organize it differently, with the hope that Jung's own purposes will be served and his writings on alchemy in particular will receive a wider and more comprehending readership.

37. "PSYCHOLOGY AND ALCHEMY"

Volume 12 of the *Collected Works*, with its extensive illustrations and excellent introduction, was written by Jung with a general readership in mind. Yet only the most erudite general reader could really tackle this volume head on. Jung's idea was to provide a kind of *apologia* for alchemy, presenting a solid block of data in the form of a fairly lengthy dream series from an individual analysis and then drawing together extensive amplificatory, symbolic parallels from the wide-ranging body of alchemical literature. His point was that alchemical imagery survives today in the individual soul because of its source in the collective unconscious. Unfortunately, despite Jung's good intentions, his organization of this volume results in throwing the uninitiated reader head first into a morass of personal and archetypal imagery with very little in the way of conceptual anchoring. Furthermore, the extensive scholarly apparatus and the entrancing visual imagery provide potent distraction to a text already packed with archetypal images.

The suggested readings here are meant to provide one first with a conceptual anchor in the form of Jung's intention in writing this book, contained in part 1, the introduction, and then a brief exposure to the fundamentals of alchemical thought and writing, in chapters 1 through 4 of part 3, "Religious Ideas in Alchemy." These chapters present certain concepts and terms common to alchemists, set forth Jung's ideas on how and what the alchemists were projecting onto their material, and give a sense of how the alchemists conceived of their work and its beginnings. These chapters will illustrate quite well how pervasive the tendency was to personify the various procedures and substances within alchemical operations, and the various psychological discussions Jung interlaces with this frequently image-dense material demonstrate Jung's interest in and use for alchemical symbolism within psychology.

The two particular images Jung explicates in this volume are of a decidedly religious character: the so-called lapis-Christ parallel and the symbol of the unicorn, treated in chapters 5 and 6 of part 3. The lapis, or stone, was an image standing for the mystico-chemical result of the alchemical work, that which the various complex procedures were intended to produce physically and spiritually. Jung is concerned with noting how the descriptions of this *lapis philosophorum*, the philosophers' stone, have undeniable parallels with descriptions of the nature and function of the Christ figure in Christianity. Likewise, his exploration and amplification of the symbol of the unicorn is carried out with the intention of drawing explicit parallels to Christian imagery. By suggesting that one read this general material on alchemy first and only afterward the modern dream series, which Jung presents as part 2, my hope is that one will then begin to recognize on one's own the alchemical themes and motifs within these dreams, rather than find oneself lost in a labyrinth of meaningless, unconnected imagery.

Jung's *Dream Analysis,* a previously unpublished seminar Jung gave on dream interpretation in Zurich once only available for consultation in Jung institutes throughout the world, is now available to the general public. This seminar aids in interpreting the dream series presented in *Psychology and Alchemy,* for it is the same patient whose dreams are discussed in both works. Marie-Louise von Franz wrote two indispensable introductions to Jung and alchemy. Equally useful is Edward Edinger's *Anatomy of the Psyche,* in which each stage of the alchemical process is examined separately for its psychological symbolism.

To Begin

Part 1, "Introduction to the Religious and Psychological Problems of Alchemy," pp. 1–37.

Part 3, "Religious Ideas in Alchemy," chap. 1, "Basic Concepts in Alchemy," pp. 225–241, chap. 2, "The Psychic Nature of the Alchemical Work," pp. 242–287, chap. 3, "The Work," pp. 288–316, chap. 4, "The Prima Materia," pp. 317–344.

To Go Deeper

Part 3, "Religious Ideas in Alchemy," chap. 5, "The Lapis-Christ Parallel," pp. 345–431, chap. 6, "Alchemical Symbolism in the History of Religion," pp. 432–471.

Part 2, "Individual Dream Symbolism in Relation to Alchemy," pp. 39–223.

Secondary Sources

Jung, C. G. *Dream Analysis: Notes of the Seminar Given in 1928–1930.* Princeton: Princeton University Press, 1984.

Von Franz, Marie-Louise. *Alchemy: Introduction to the Symbolism and the Psychology.* Toronto: Inner City Books, 1980.

Von Franz, Marie-Louise. *Alchemical Active Imagination.* Dallas: Spring Publications, 1979. Boston: Shambhala Publications, 1997.

Edinger, Edward. *The Anatomy of the Psyche: Alchemical Symbolism in Psychotherapy.* La Salle, Ill.: Open Court, 1985.

38. "MYSTERIUM CONIUNCTIONIS"

As with *Psychology and Alchemy*, certain parts of this work, volume 14 of the *Collected Works*, are less abstruse than others, since as usual Jung jumps right into the thick of things. The general intention of this book, Jung's last published work, was to examine in depth the central problem of alchemy, namely the union of opposites from which the alchemists imagined would emerge the goal of the alchemical procedure, a goal variously described in typical alchemical fashion as gold, the lapis, the *hierosgamos*, or incestuous sacred marriage, and so on. Thus Jung examines the host of imagery in the alchemical literature which describes the various opposites to be united, sets of opposites that the alchemists personified chiefly as masculine/feminine pairs. Three such masculine/feminine pairs within alchemy—Sol and Luna (Sun and Moon), Rex and Regina (King and Queen), and Adam and Eve—are the major focus of Jung's examination.

Because alchemy was largely a men's occupation, much of the material centers on the masculine half of these pairs of opposites, especially Rex (who is explicated by way of an alchemical poem by Sir George Ripley) and Adam (who is examined in relationship to Jewish mystical literature). The sole exception here is the extensive section on Luna, which is both evocative and seminal for later Jungian writers on femininity. Subsequent to examining the individual members of these oppositional pairs, Jung goes on to examine the images and sym-

170

bols that pertain to the *mysterium coniunctionis* itself, the mystery of union, how it is produced, what it appears to be, its spiritual and psychological meaning.

While this book is an excellent example of Jung's method of symbol amplication, the task of reading it is made daunting by Jung's far-ranging allusions to mythology, folktales, Christian theology, and medieval philosophy. Likewise, the elusive quality of the symbolism within alchemy does not make reading this material any easier (for example, the discussion on Luna leads into a symbolic examination of salt, the Red Sea, dog imagery, quicksilver, and number symbolism), and again, the scholarly apparatus required to document and translate the Latin and Greek of these ancient texts provides yet another hurdle to easy perusal. When Jung concentrates on particular texts, as with the Enigma of Bologna in part 2 or Ripley's *Cantilena* in part 4, the discussions take on a more logical, less amplificatory character, because they are anchored to a particular text or question. The prose of *Mysterium Coniunctionis* ebbs and flows, therefore, reaching difficult knots of imaginal density which then resolve themselves into more lucid and free-flowing expositions of psychological and alchemical symbolism. The challenge in reading this type of book is to follow the thread of the symbol amplification, to see the way in which one image is related to the next, developing, changing, progressing, and yet consistently the same and consistently interconnected at the core.

Again, the readings suggested here are organized so that those parts that are clearest and easiest to read come first, followed by the more dense or difficult. In the case of *Mysterium Coniunctionis,* the personification of the opposites, as presented in parts 3 through 5, allows for a clearer and more grounded exposition of the alchemical concepts and provides a better foothold on the first two parts, which are a bit far-flung without anchoring images. Jung's discussion of the Enigma of Bologna, a medieval stone inscription, is both lively and useful in giving the reader a sense of the place of projection within alchemical interpretations. Once these opposites are known and have become "familiars," then the last part of the book, on their union, or *coniunctio*, makes most sense. Edward Edinger's lecture transcript is a unique and very useful guided tour of its own through this dense, fascinating text and is highly recommended as a way into this work.

To Begin

Part 1, "The Components of the Coniunctio," chap. 1, "The Opposites," pp. 3–6.

Part 3, "The Personification of Opposites," pp. 89–257.

Part 4, "Rex and Regina," pp. 258–381.

Part 5, "Adam and Eve," pp. 382–456.

Part 2, "The Paradoxa," chap. 3, "The Enigma of Bologna," pp. 56–88.

To Go Deeper

Part 1, "The Components of the Coniunctio," chap. 2, "The Quaternio and the Mediating Role of Mercurius," chap. 3, "The Orphan, the Widow and the Moon," and chap. 4, "Alchemy and Manichaeism," pp. 6–37.

Part 2, "The Paradoxa," chap. 1, "The Arcane Substance and the Point," and chap. 2, "The Scintilla," pp. 42–56.

Part 6, "The Conjunction," pp. 457–553.

Epilogue, pp. 554–556.

Secondary Source

Edinger, Edward F. *The Mysterium Lectures: A Journey through C. G. Jung's* Mysterium Coniunctionis. Toronto: Inner City Books, 1995.

39. "ALCHEMICAL STUDIES"

Volume 13 of the *Collected Works* brings together five studies on alchemical subjects. Occupying the middle position in the three volumes of the *Collected Works* on alchemy, *Alchemical Studies* is generally more comprehensible than *Mysterium Coniunctionis* or *Psychology and Alchemy* because of the specific focus of each of the pieces. Without having read the other two, more extensive volumes on alchemy, however, these discussions may appear without context and therefore be superficially understood. Thus it is suggested that one do the hard but important legwork of reading *Mysterium Coniunctionis* and *Psychology and Alchemy* first, before delving into these more focused essays.

While the five essays indeed treat the topic of alchemy, the first, *Commentary on "The Secret of the Golden Flower,"* has to do with a Chinese alchemical text; the other four stay within Jung's major field of expertise, the Western alchemical tradition. Furthermore, for obvious reasons, one ought to read Wilhelm's translation of this Chinese text (or Baynes' English translation of Wilhelm's German translation) before turning to Jung's commentary. Of these five essays, therefore, I suggest saving the first until the end, since it provides an excellent counterpoint to the enormous mass of Jung's work on Western alchemical thought and is one of Jung's clearest and most significant statements on the relationship between Eastern spirituality and Western psychology.

Of the remaining four essays, two consist largely of examinations of particular texts, *The Visions of Zosimos* and *De Vita Longa* (On Long Life), by the Swiss alchemist Paracelsus, and

173

two focus on particularly important alchemical symbols, Mercurius and the philosophical tree. The essays on Zosimos and
Paracelsus will be refreshingly lucid for those readers who have
studied Jung's longer works on alchemy and will acquaint these
readers with a deeper and more detailed view of particular systems of alchemical symbolism. Both Zosimos, in his reported
visions, and Paracelsus, in his writings, use many images common to alchemical thought but provide idiosyncratic and at
times illuminating variations of standard alchemical systems.

With *The Spirit Mercurius* and *The Philosophical Tree,* Jung
repeats the technique he used in *Psychology and Alchemy,* beginning these two studies with nonalchemical material—a folktale
about Mercurius and case material on trees, respectively—to
introduce the alchemical material that follows. In the case of
The Spirit Mercurius, this technique succeeds largely because the
folktale and Jung's interpretation of it are short and to the
point. However, the series of clinical tree images in *The Philosophical Tree* may have the same effect as the extensive dream
series in *Psychology and Alchemy:* throwing the unsuspecting
reader head first into a plethora of tree symbols without sufficient cognitive orientation. For those who have read most of
Jung's work on alchemy, this essay might be read as written,
but for readers unfamiliar with the imagery of alchemy, similar
advice is given: One should read the second part of *The Philosophical Tree* first and save the clinical material for last, when
Jung's intention will be clear and when one will be more familiar with the symbolism in question.

Since both the Chinese and the Paracelsan texts concern
themselves with the question of long life, these essays, in a
sense, support Jung's contention that alchemy was not exclusively concerned with the *ars aurifera,* mere gold-making, but
with questions of spiritual and psychological urgency. In this
context, Jung's study of Mercurius, one of the most abiding
and central symbolic entities throughout the seventeen-hun-

dred-year history and development of alchemical thought, en-
lightens the full complexity of the alchemical program and its
relationship to Christian dogmatic dominance. These essays,
therefore, represent important contributions to Jung's body of
work on the psychological and spiritual relevance of alchemical
symbolism.

To Begin

> *The Visions of Zosimos,* CW 13, pp. 57–108.
> *Paracelsus as a Spiritual Phenomenon,* CW 13, pp. 109–189.
> *The Spirit Mercurius,* CW 13, pp. 191–250.
> *The Philosophical Tree,* CW 13, pp. 251–349.

To Go Deeper

> *Commentary on "The Secret of the Golden Flower,* CW 13, pp. 1–56.

Related Works

> "Paracelsus," CW 15, pp. 3–12.
> "Paracelsus the Physician," CW 15, pp. 13–20.
> "Richard Wilhelm: In Memoriam," CW 15, pp. 53–62.

Secondary Sources

> Wilhelm, Richard, trans. *The Secret of the Golden Flower: A Chinese
> Book of Life.* New York: Harcourt Brace Jovanovich, 1931.

40. "AION"

Aion is the second of a pair of books devoted to specific archetypes. Unlike volume 9, part 1, which examines a number of different archetypes, the sole subject of *Aion* is the archetype of the Self. The title comes from the Greek word for eon or age, and, as Jung points out in the foreword, it is meant to refer to the age of Christianity and the collective psychic development that Christian symbolism represents. Jung examines Christian symbolism, especially Christ and the symbol of the fish so closely associated with Christ, as a way of gaining a clearer view of what he terms the Self, the God image within the soul, the archetype of wholeness and fulfillment.

For readers familiar with Jung's writings, therefore, the first part of the book will present few difficulties. Jung sets forth in brief form his concepts of the ego, the shadow, and the anima/animus. The latter pair is called here the syzygy, an astronomical and astrological term for a conjunction of planets. Jung often applied this term to the anima/animus to indicate the union of opposites which these intrapsychic, contrasexual archetypes represent for the individual, how a *coniunctio* in the process of individuation would lead one to a more conscious connection to wholeness itself, the Self. Jung then goes on to examine the Self, the archetype that lies behind the God symbolism of religion, and how the figure of Christ is a Self symbol within Christianity. In these sections, what comes through most clearly and in most detail is Jung's dissatisfaction with the way in which dogmatic Christianity very early on dismissed the reality of evil in the world, explaining evil away as a lack of good-

176

ness (*privatio boni*), instead of understanding that evil and good are coequal forces in psychological experience. Thus, the Christ symbol within Christianity is split into a Christ/Antichrist pair, a situation that, from a psychological point of view, represents an unsatisfactory resolution of the problem of wholeness as a union of opposites. Therefore, what has been hinted at or only briefly mentioned in Jung's other writings on Christianity is here fully developed: Jung believed that Christian symbolism does not do full justice to the real psychological forces within the soul and so does not provide a workable way to psychological wholeness unless supplemented by a fuller appreciation of the presence of evil in the soul and in the world.

The reading gets more difficult when Jung examines the symbolism of the fishes as a symbol for Christ, winding his way through astrological material on the fish in chapters 6 and 7, as well as pagan and comparative religious material on the fish symbol in chapters 8 and 9, with the intention of bringing to light how the fish is a symbol of the light/dark duality inherent in the Christian conception of Christ as a symbol of wholeness. Chapters 10 and 11 go on to detail the nature of the fish symbol within alchemical writings, summed up in the excellent and quite readable chapter 12, "Background to the Psychology of Christian Alchemical Symbolism." Because these discussions are actually amplifications of fish symbolism, Jung casts his net wide, catching symbols related to the fish in various ways: the jellyfish and its spherical luminosity, the idea of the remora as magnet, the relationship between serpent and fish, the Behemoth and Leviathan of Jewish tradition, and various conceptions of the zodiacal Pisces and its place within astrological belief systems.

Then Jung uses the "ambivalence of the fish symbol" to dig further and deeper into the writings of Gnosticism, whose relationship to Christian theology yields many important but ignored psychological facts about the experience and symbolism of Christ as the Self. Gnostic conceptions of evil and matter form a marked contrast to the overspiritualization so characteristic of orthodox Christianity, and therefore Jung looks in great detail at various Gnostic beliefs and symbols to supplement the orthodox Christian formulations he has found so unsatisfactory. Unfortunately for the uninitiated reader, Gnosticism is neither easier nor more organized than the body of alchemical writings, and Jung brings little structure or organization to his discussion since his intention is to find symbolic parallels, not codify or theorize.

The last chapter of the book, "The Structure and Dynamics of the Self," attempts a synthesis of the foregoing mass of symbolism and suggests a structural model of the Self, resembling an eight-sided crystal. Jung's intention here is to find a way to organize the pieces of the personality, symbolized by the various symbolic or mythic figures, into a structure that relates them all, one to another, while remaining faithful to the tension of opposites inherent in the various pairs. Thus this crystal, built on a square in which four pairs stand in complementary relationship to one another, reaches up to a point of conscious unity and down to a point of unconscious wholeness. Other symbolic figures representing wholeness, such as the squared circle, the parallelogram, and other crystalline structures, are also examined here. Whether executed successfully or unsuccessfully, Jung's intention is to schematize and organize material that, as the reader has undoubtedly seen, shifts, moves, and wiggles with all the ungraspability of a literal fish. Obviously, these models are not to be taken as anything but that: models to help one conceptualize how certain aspects of one's inner symbolic life may stand in relation to every other.

Like the alchemical writings, this book is perhaps most profitably read a little at a time. However, unlike many of Jung's alchemical writings, *Aion* has a consistent focus—the connection between the Self, Christ, and the symbolism of the fish—

and is organized in a way that is not initially off-putting. The richness of the imagery and the overwhelming scholarship, nevertheless, make the book more an object of repeated study than a simply read exposition. Its importance in the *Collected Works* cannot be stressed enough, since it contains Jung's longest statement of his ideas on and difficulties with Christian symbolism from a psychological point of view.

Continuing its publication of a series of transcribed lectures and seminars by Edinger, Inner City Books has issued yet another unique guide to readers wishing an entrée into these furthest reaches of Jung's psychology.

Secondary Source

Edinger, Edward F. The *Aion Lectures: Exploring the Self in C. G. Jung's* Aion. Toronto: Inner City Books, 1996.

BIBLIOGRAPHY

The Collected Works of C. G. Jung

1. Psychiatric Studies

On the Psychology and Pathology of So-Called Occult Phenomena

On Hysterical Misreading

Cryptomnesia

On Manic Mood Disorder

A Case of Hysterical Stupor in a Prisoner in Detention

On Simulated Insanity

A Medical Opinion on a Case of Simulated Insanity

A Third and Final Opinion of Two Contradictory Psychiatric Diagnoses

On the Psychological Diagnosis of Facts

2. Experimental Researches

STUDIES IN WORD ASSOCIATION

The Associations of Normal Subjects (by Jung and F. Riklin)

An Analysis of the Associations of an Epileptic

The Reaction-Time Ratio in the Association Experiment

Experimental Observations on the Faculty of Memory

Psychoanalysis and Association Experiments

The Psychological Diagnosis of Evidence

Association, Dream, and Hysterical Symptom

The Transformation of Libido

The Origin of the Hero

Symbols of the Mother and of Rebirth

The Battle for Deliverance from the Mother

The Dual Mother

The Sacrifice

Epilogue

Appendix: The Miller Fantasies

6. Psychological Types

Introduction

The Problem of Types in the History of Classical and Medieval Thought

Schiller's Ideas on the Type Problem

The Apollonian and the Dionysian

The Type Problem in Human Character

The Type Problem in Poetry

The Type Problem in Psychopathology

The Type Problem in Aesthetics

The Type Problem in Modern Philosophy

The Type Problem in Biography

General Description of the Types

Definitions

Epilogue

Four Papers on Psychological Typology (1913, 1925, 1931, 1936)

7. Two Essays on Analytical Psychology

On the Psychology of the Unconscious

The Relations between the Ego and the Unconscious

Appendices:
New Paths in Psychology
The Structure of the Unconscious

8. *The Structure and Dynamics of the Psyche*
    On Psychic Energy
    The Transcendent Function
    A Review of the Complex Theory
    The Significance of Constitution and Heredity in Psychology
    Psychological Factors Determining Human Behaviour
    Instinct and the Unconscious
    The Structure of the Psyche
    On the Nature of the Psyche
    General Aspects of Dream Psychology
    On the Nature of Dreams
    The Psychological Foundations of Belief in Spirits
    Spirit and Life
    Basic Postulates of Analytical Psychology
    Analytical Psychology and *Weltanschauung*
    The Real and the Surreal
    The Stages of Life
    The Soul and Death
    Synchronicity: An Acausal Connecting Principle
    Appendix: On Synchronicity

9. *Part I: The Archetypes and the Collective Unconscious*
    Archetypes of the Collective Unconscious
    The Concept of the Collective Unconscious
    Concerning the Archetypes, with Special Reference to the Anima
        Concept
    Psychological Aspects of the Mother Archetype

11. Psychology and Religion: West and East

WESTERN RELIGION